THE
MYSTICAL WAY
IN THE
FOURTH GOSPEL

THE
MYSTICAL WAY
IN THE
FOURTH GOSPEL

Crossing Over into God

L. WILLIAM COUNTRYMAN

Fortress Press   Philadelphia

Library of Congress Cataloging-in-Publication Data

Countryman, L. William.
  The mystical way in the fourth Gospel.

  Includes index.
  1. Bible. N.T. John—Criticism, interpretation, etc. I. Title.
BS2615.2.C69 1987   226'.507   86–45913
ISBN 0–8006–1949–8

2651J86   Printed in the United States of America   1–1949

Magistro Meo
Robert M. Grant
Magnis Cum Gratiis

CONTENTS

ACKNOWLEDGMENTS

The understanding of John's Gospel presented here has been more than a decade in taking shape, having taken its rise in a course with Robert M. Grant early in 1973. Although he may not recognize it in its developed form, it is meet and right that it should be dedicated to a teacher from whom I have learned so much, above all to pursue my own vision with all the energy and care at my command.

My thanks go also to students at Brite Divinity School and the Church Divinity School of the Pacific in the Graduate Theological Union, Berkeley, California, for their tolerance, good humor, and encouragement while I worked through these ideas aloud. Among my students, I owe particular thanks to Leigh Bond, Ann Richards, and Joel Aurand. It was Scott Sinclair who told me I was through thinking out loud and should begin to write. Margo Delaney has been an enthusiastic and indefatigable friend to both the work and the author as the manuscript took shape. Five colleagues and friends undertook to read an early draft and gave me much helpful guidance: William Baird, Michael Blecker, Jerry Brown, Howard Miller, and Howard Stone. If the reader finds lingering faults, they should be put down to the author's short-sightedness and even occasional stubbornness. Finally, my thanks to John A. Hollar of Fortress Press for help in clarifying the book's audience and forms.

While the writing of the book has been an act of scholarship for me, it has equally been an act of prayer. I hope that, in the present state of our hermeneutics, those realities will not seem to be at war with each other.

Berkeley, California　　　　　　　　　　　L. WM. COUNTRYMAN
St. Hilarion's Day, 1985

INTRODUCTION

The purpose of the present work is to offer a new reading of John's Gospel as a sustained literary whole—a reading which sees the Gospel as focused on progress toward mystical union in the person of Jesus. Since the word "mystical" is used in a variety of senses, it may be helpful to define how I am using it here. I take it to describe an experience of things or persons outside myself as direct and unmediated as my experience of myself is. At one level, this may be an experience of the order of the cosmos and of my place in it, in which case it is called "mystical enlightenment." At another level it may be an experience of full knowledge of another specific being, in which case it is called "mystical union." (Union may be understood as implying a complete dissolution of the human who enters into it, or may appear as the complete opening of two realities into one another. The latter interpretation is the more common within Christianity, often expressed through the metaphor of sexual intercourse.) In practice, it may not always be possible to distinguish enlightenment sharply from union; but I believe that John treats the former as prelude to the latter.

In the following chapters, I shall argue that the Gospel of John is structured according to the experience of the believer, whose very existence emerges from and depends on the primeval union of God and Logos and whose goal is the union of believing humanity in and with Father and Son. Jesus, who is Logos and Son, is the only opening humanity has upon the absolute reality of God. This reality is ours merely by our existing, but may also become ours in a greater sense by our believing. Writing for a

1

Christian audience, John presents the mystical path as the continuation of their existing religious experience. Conversion, baptism, and reception of the Eucharist lead on without a break (though not by any sort of inevitability) to mystical enlightenment and union. This union is itself tasted in this life, but reaches its consummation only in the life of the world to come. John's Gospel functions not only to sketch out this "program" but actually to encourage the committed reader along the path through conundrums whose solution moves one toward enlightenment—and also through models, warnings, and a theology that grounds the whole process.

To suggest that the Fourth Gospel is mystical is nothing new. As early as the second century, Clement of Alexandria, in an effort to capture its distinctive quality, referred to it as the "spiritual" Gospel. Its author soon came to be called John the *Theologos* (in English, the "Divine" or the "Theologian"), a term which, in antiquity, suggested the mystic rather than the professional or academic theologian of today. By the Middle Ages, the eagle had become the emblem of this Gospel, because its strong flight seemed to take it near the sun, God's image in the material world. The first two commentaries on the book, by Heracleon in the second century and Origen in the third, both seem to assume that the Gospel is mystical in some sense. By the time these commentaries were written, however, the Fourth Gospel had already become "scripture"—almost tantamount at the time to "a collection of oracles." An analytical process of interpretation, one that separated the problems of one verse or paragraph from those of the next, had already set in; and it was difficult to read the book as a sustained, organic whole. Origen approached this ideal and was clearly aware of the relative distribution of materials in John and the other three New Testament Gospels; yet, his enormous, incomplete commentary does not give us a view of the whole.[1]

In more recent times, most scholarly investigation of the book has focused on issues other than mysticism. Scholars have studied the book's historical tradition, its affiliations in the history of religions, its philosophical and theological relationships, its place in the history of early Christianity, its language, its internal history of authorship and editing, and so on. One might find reason to suggest that modern analytical scholarship has made us uneasy about studying the specifically religious or mystical wellsprings of early Christianity. This sense of unease has been reinforced by factors not strictly academic, such as a historic Protestant antagonism toward mysticism, resurgent in our century in Barthianism and neo-orthodoxy, and apologetic concerns for making Christianity intelligible in a supposedly postreligious era.[2]

This is not to say that John's mysticism has received no notice whatever in modern times. Baron von Hugel, writing on John in the eleventh edition of the *Encyclopaedia Britannica*, described the Gospel as embodying an "elemental mode of apprehension and root truth," a mysticism which he felt must no longer be very attractive in the modern world. C. H. Dodd made a major contribution toward sorting out relationships between Johannine and Hellenistic mysticisms, capably seconded by David L. Mealand. William J. Fulco offered a treatment of John's mystical theology arranged topically. All these treatments share the presupposition that mysticism is interesting to the student of John for other than purely literary reasons—as cultural background or as a predilection of the author or as a style of theology implied in the work.[3]

Only one modern critic, as far as I know, goes beyond this presupposition to suggest that mysticism might not only provide the milieu of the Fourth Gospel, but might even be its principal focus. This was Evelyn Underhill, not a New Testament scholar, but the century's great student of mysticism. In a chapter of her book *The Mystic Way*, she argued that mystic experience was the principal source of John's Gospel—of its overall viewpoint and even, to a degree, of the narratives themselves. She then went on to say:

> Although it is unlikely that so subjective and poetic—so "inspired"—a book was systematically planned, yet the idea by which its writer was possessed, his one deep vision and conviction, does unfold itself in a certain order.

Underhill suggested that the book was organized in terms of mystical experience, which she understood to consist, more or less invariably, of three stages: purgative, illuminative, and unitive. While her application of this idea remained somewhat vague and impressionistic, it is a forerunner of the basic premise of the present work: the Gospel of John is mystical not incidentally (in terms of its background or implied theology), but essentially (in its basic literary purpose and structure). The mystical path, in other words, is the point of the Gospel's presentation of Jesus.[4]

The present study, in concerning itself with the Gospel of John as a literary whole, makes something of a break with the scholarly tradition. Modern New Testament scholarship has often preferred analytical modes of study—the isolation of specific problems which are dealt with individually and only then brought together to form a larger, composite picture. This has been a fruitful method of approach, but it has its limits. In a work of literary art, such as any one of the four New Testament Gospels, the meaning of individual parts is determined largely by their organic relation to the whole. Any scholarship that works from literary evidence, even if its own questions and interests are not literary, must always take account of this reality.

Interest in literary-critical methods has shown a resurgence recently in New Testament studies. It is not surprising, however, to find that the more analytical models developed by our colleagues in other literary fields are the ones that have captured our attention. One can readily find analyses of New Testament texts in the modes of source analysis, audience criticism, or structuralist interpretation. These may often be useful, but they do not contend seriously with the basic problem—the need to grasp a work as a concrete and organic whole.

The method of the present work—if "method" is not too grand a term—is quite different. I have assumed that the individual word or verse or paragraph has very little meaning in and of itself. Or, to put the same point in another way, it is replete with meanings, from among which one is powerless to choose without some higher guiding principle. This principle, ultimately, cannot be found outside the literary work itself. It will always be necessary for the student of an ancient text to know as much as possible about the text's own geographical, cultural, and historical setting and how it differed from that of today. Yet, with the ancient text as with the modern, there remains the element of the unique and individual which sets each work apart, makes it different from all others, and permeates it in the form of a wholeness that belongs to this text and to no other.

How does one reach toward this literary whole? In a short lyric or anecdote or epigram, the whole can be grasped in what seems like a single moment of attention. That is no longer possible with an extended narrative, even a fairly brief one like the Gospel of John. Here we must find other ways of moving from the smaller parts that can be grasped to the enormously complex whole that does not offer itself directly. Yet, these must not be analytical methods, which would only isolate part from whole.

I suggest that the movement toward the literary whole proceeds in this way. One comes to the work, intentionally or not, with various interpretive impedimenta: hypotheses and presuppositions about what is central and what is not. Some of these may be appropriate presuppositions and others not, but one does not know in advance which are which. What one does know is that there is much in the literary work that is puzzling on whatever presuppositions one brings. These points of perplexity are the points of entry.

The worst thing the reader can do is to skate over these troublesome spots or to explain them away in order to save one's hypothesis. The next worst thing is to separate them from one another in the hope that dividing them will make them easier to conquer. To be sure, some sources of our puzzlement will prove to be resolved by historical elucidation of the ancient context of the work; but we do not know in advance where this will prove to be the case. The best course is to move through the points of perplexity to a deep immersion into the whole literary work, reading and rereading it until it becomes, with all its alien and irritant qualities, a part of the reader. Once we have incorporated the work thus, in a way that acknowledges the inadequacy of our understanding of it, we are ready to seek a new vision of the whole that will resolve our perplexities by setting them in a new relationship in which they make sense.

In the present study, which has gone on intermittently for more than a decade, I entered the text through two particular points of perplexity, both of importance in determining the literary structure of the Gospel of John. The first of these is the high frequency of what I call the "inappropriate response" in this Gospel. I mean by this instances when an interlocutor approaches Jesus with a question or leading statement and Jesus replies with what at first seems to be a non sequitur. For example, at the Last Supper one of the disciples asks, "Sir, what's happened that you're going to show yourself to us and not to the cosmos?" Jesus replies, "If anyone loves me, he'll keep my word. And my father will love him, and we'll come to him and make a place to stay with him" (14:22–23). At first sight, the response is quite unrelated to the question. If such responses are not mere clumsiness on the part of author or editor, as has sometimes been suggested,[5] one must ask after their function. To the idle or casual reader, they may be mere irritations; for the reader committed to fathoming the Gospel, however, they have the effect of slowing one's pace, making one less self-confident, and compelling reflection.

Such effects might serve a variety of purposes. In Plato's dialogues, Socrates is sometimes portrayed as leaping ahead of his companions and expressing a conclusion that startles the others and entices them into intellectual reexamination of the subject. John, however, does not use the inappropriate response in quite that way—at least, not explicitly. John's use of the device is more closely akin to that of another ancient work, the little treatise *On Rebirth* which forms the thirteenth tractate of the *Corpus Hermeticum*. Here, the inappropriate response is used to force the reader to break with ordinary straight-line reasoning and struggle for a new world view in which question and answer do match.[6] The achievement of such a breakthrough is an instance of enlightenment—not an increase of knowledge but a radical reshuffling and reenvisioning of what is already known. *On Rebirth* is, in fact, explicitly dedicated to producing just such results, though only with some few initiates who are properly prepared for its use. This raises the question whether John's Gospel might not also have had a kind of mystical enlightenment as its goal, with the instances of inappropriate response spurring the reader on toward a more adequate vision of reality. John's Gospel, however, is not so clearly adapted to such a purpose as *On Rebirth*. The latter is a dialogue, in which the god Hermes Trismegistus leads his son Tat toward the moment of enlightenment (here called "rebirth"); the subsequent reader can take the place of Tat easily enough in order to follow the process of initiation. John, however, has written a narrative about past events.

At this point, the second perplexing aspect of John's Gospel becomes important for me: John seems to have a strongly ambivalent attitude toward the Christian sacraments of Baptism and the Eucharist, so much so that it has a critical effect on the literary structure of his book.[7] The Gospel has the external form of a book about the life and ministry of Jesus; yet, in the matter of the sacraments, it violates this form. The other three New Testament Gospels suggest that the baptism of Jesus by John the Baptist and Jesus' own institution of the Lord's Supper just before he was arrested were both important elements in the earliest traditions about Jesus' life and ministry. In the case of the Lord's Supper,

Paul confirms this in 1 Cor. 11:23–26. John never mentions either of these traditions; and yet, he presents us with passages so closely related to them that one can scarcely suppose that he was ignorant of them. Why would he pass over these narratives in their proper places?

To add to the perplexity, John further gives the impression of intense ambivalence about the sacraments as such. The Jesus who tells Nicodemus, in 3:5–8, that he must be born of water and wind (or spirit) goes on to tell him in 3:12 that this is only an earthly thing, not a heavenly one. The Jesus who declares that "The one who chews my flesh and drinks my blood has everlasting life" (6:54) goes on to say, "The spirit is what gives life; the flesh does no good at all" (6:63). The ambiguous picture that thus emerges suggests that our author saw the sacramental rites as both essential and inadequate. This is an intelligible position for a mystic, who may well see external rites as a means to other ends. In itself, however, this does not explain why he would suppress the familiar narratives. The whole complex of sacramental references begins to make sense only when we attend to their location within the larger framework of the Gospel.

On purely narrative principles, the baptism of Jesus would belong in chapter 1 and the institution of the Lord's Supper in chapter 13. Yet, most water imagery and other allusions to baptism are found in chapters 2—5, while language and images apposite to the Eucharist are largely limited to chapter 6. The concentration of these matters just here makes no sense on historical principles and is far from necessary in a narrative of Jesus' ministry. It makes very good sense, however, in terms of the life of John's original Christian reader. This reader will usually, given the circumstances of John's time, have been an adult convert, initiated into the Christian community by a rite consisting of Baptism and Eucharist, and continuing to participate in the community's eucharistic meal. Having recognized, in chapters 1—6, her previous religious experience, she is then prepared, in the reading of the Gospel, to follow further along the path toward mystical enlightenment and union in the subsequent pages.

In this way, my two sets of perplexities have served as points of entry, suggesting that it will be worth looking at the Gospel of John, from a literary-critical point of view, as embodying a mystical world view and purpose. It is not possible—and this book will not attempt—to produce a "proof" of such an interpretation.

If the "whole" of a literary work could be abstracted from the work itself and reduced to a sentence or two or to a chart, then perhaps one could think of "proving" it. As easily hope to reduce a living human being to a line or two. . . . What is possible is rather to *show* others the whole one has seen by reading the book with them and pointing out how things that perplex the reader on other hypotheses fall into place and make sense, given this notion of the whole.

Although the present work seeks to explore these issues primarily through literary means, it will be useful, particularly for the reader familiar with Johannine studies, to locate this study in relation to important textual and historical issues. First, as regards the text itself, I assume that the last chapter of John's Gospel (chap. 21) as we now have it is an appendix and not a part of the book's original plan. Chapter 20 provides an appropriate conclusion to the whole work, while chapter 21 seems preoccupied with the specific question of the theological interpretation of the author's death. The appendix must have been part of the Gospel as it was first published, since it is found in all copies; but the hand which placed a final stamp on chapters 1—20 either did not write it or else added it subsequently. Accordingly, I have provided a translation of chapter 21 in an appendix, but have not dealt with it in the main body of this work.

Another passage that I have also removed to an appendix is the story of the woman taken in adultery (John 7:53—8:11). It is poorly represented in the manuscript tradition, where it appears in a variety of places in the Gospels of John and Luke. I should rue its loss from the New Testament canon for reasons of its own intrinsic merits; but it can scarcely be considered a part of John for purposes of literary analysis.

It is possible that there was a history of various drafts or editions before John 1—20 reached its present form. There is no scholarly consensus about the details of the matter, however, and I think it is fair to say that if the final shaper of these chapters was not the original author, he or she is more important in any case. This final shaper is the person I refer to as the "author" and as "John"—the person's traditional name, which could easily be correct. The issue of this person's relationship to the Beloved Disciple does not seem to me to be critical for what I am doing here.[8]

The individuality of the work, as compared with the other New Testament Gospels or with Paul, suggests a highly original mind at work, perhaps in a somewhat isolated or marginal Christian community. While the history of this community is hard to trace, the emerging consensus that it consisted mainly of Hellenistic Jewish Christians living in close proximity to and in conflict with non-Christian Jews seems sound. I follow Kenneth Grayston in thinking that the First Epistle of John represents an earlier stage in the life of this community. The theological tensions evident there have matured and come to fruition in the theology of the Gospel, which seeks to bring together the insistence on the historical Jesus found in 1 John with the interest of the charismatic "opponents" in that epistle in immediate religious experience.[9]

The translation of John's Gospel presented here is my own, made from the United Bible Societies Greek New Testament, third edition.[10] Where I have departed from the judgment of its editors, I explain my reasons in the notes. Apart from such necessary matters, however, I have kept notes to a minimum, for the crucial argument for the thesis of this work is not so much the way it relates to recent analytical scholarship as the way it reveals the Gospel of John as a literary whole. In no way, however, do I wish to deny or ignore the enormous debt I owe to a great variety of modern scholars who have elucidated John for me.

The translation seemed necessary for several reasons. First, I want the reader to "walk through" the Gospel with me, not merely to hear isolated comments about it. Without our attending constantly to the text itself, we shall miss the opportunity to comprehend it as an organic whole. Second, my own work with John's Gospel has been based entirely on the Greek text. When I returned to English translations, I found that they were based on overall conceptions of the work which made them nearly useless for the present purpose. They sometimes unintentionally concealed what I thought it most important to reveal, since their translators had different evaluations of what was important. My translation, then, is part of my argument, though I trust that it is not unfairly biased.

In the style of the translation, I have aimed principally at two goals: to be fairly literal and to re-create some of the elements of Johannine style in English. Only the person who can read the Greek of John with some ease can hope to catch quite all that is going on literarily; by being fairly literal, I have tried to keep the translation somewhat transparent to the Greek. Some of the oddness of this translation, however, is the result not of literalism, but of the effort to find an English equivalent to Johannine style. Our convention in biblical translation has always been to seek a smooth and literate English style, one which often misrepresents the Greek of the New Testament authors. John's style is characterized by directness, a certain jerkiness, a pattern of usage that is broadly correct without being refined, a tendency to repetition, and an artificially small vocabulary. Much of John's vocabulary has since become highly charged theologically, in a way that it may not have been in his own time. I have sought to reduce the charge by avoiding most capitalization and many common English theological terms, such as "world" and "Paraclete." "Cosmos" may seem odd in place of the more familiar "world," but its very unfamiliarity may provide the reader the necessary occasion to let John's usage determine its meaning in the text.[11] In the matter of inclusivity of language, particularly as regards our inconvenient third-person singular pronouns, I have treated the Gospel as an artifact of its own age and not sought to modernize it.

Finally, some readers may wonder at times how I decided what specific texts I would comment on at length. Quite simply, I have written most about those which seemed to me to be most in need of it—that is, the texts which have particularly perplexed me in the past and which thereby occasioned this excursion into John. I hope that I have discussed whatever might seem to create difficulties for the hypothesis I am presenting here, but I doubt that I shall have noticed all the possibilities of interpretation. I will have done my work if this book provides the reader with a way to grasp the Gospel of John as a whole. I fear that a more detailed commentary would have concealed the goal toward which it pretended to move.

1

Theological
Postulates

PROLOGUE

(John 1:1-34)

In creating his Gospel, John was balancing at least three major structural concerns: (1) to preserve the outward form of a "life" of Jesus; (2) to detail, beneath this surface form, the experience of the believer in progressing toward mystical union; (3) to offer a theology which would make sense of the combination of the two. This theology is not only a literary necessity for the book, but a necessity of life for the Johannine community, which has staked its identity on the belief that the individual historical person Jesus is of decisive importance for human relationship with God.[1] John's mysticism is tied absolutely to a historical character; he must present a Christology that will justify such an improbability. What is more, one stage along the mystic way, for John, will be the kind of enlightenment by which the believer recognizes this role of Jesus—not as a theological abstraction, but as the reality of one's own existence. Thus, the theology of the Gospel of John is the keystone of an arch, which the life of Jesus and that of the believer both lean upon and support.

It is the mystic's *experience* of theology, however, that crowns the book, not intellectual theology in the abstract sense. The latter is more nearly the foundation or presupposition for the book. John begins with it, in the prologue, in an allusive way, suggesting much that is to come, yet not in such a way that one could predict what follows—or even, just at this point, understand the full significance of what is being said. The issues raised in the prologue will not disappear at the end of it. They will return again and again in different guises throughout the book and grad-

11

ually be related more and more explicitly to the believer's experience.

Oddly enough, the characteristic vocabulary of the prologue does not all carry over into the rest of the work. We shall hear again of "life" and "light" and "cosmos" and "dark." But "logos" does not recur in the peculiar sense given it here (except, as I shall suggest, for allusive plays upon it at 10:35 and 14:24); instead, the being here called "logos" will always, later, be called "son." Nor shall we hear again the language of "becoming flesh" and "tenting among us" or the phrase "lamb of God." The peculiarity of its vocabulary thus makes the prologue stand somewhat apart from the rest of the Gospel. Some have explained this by supposing that the author has incorporated an originally independent hymn (which might have consisted of vv. 1–5, 10–11, 15)[2] which did not reflect his own linguistic usage, or that the prologue (at least vv. 1–18) might be a later addition to the book. Without seeking to resolve such questions, I think it will appear throughout the present work that the prologue actually provides the necessary presuppositions for understanding the Gospel as a whole. However idiosyncratic its language, it is thoroughly coherent in thought with the rest of John's book and forms an integral part of it.

As the title of the present chapter indicates, I am defining the prologue as consisting of the first thirty-four verses of John 1. Those familiar with Johannine scholarship will recognize that this is unusual, for the term "prologue" as normally used refers only to 1:1–18. Since there is also a sharp stylistic break after 1:18, it may seem hard to justify any different usage. I should argue, however, that weighty considerations justify my present approach. First, in terms of the conventions of biography, one must regard any material regarding origin and identity of the subject as essentially prefatory to that person's arrival on the scene as an adult. In John's Gospel, Jesus arrives as an actual participant in the narrative only in 1:35. Everything up to that point is therefore preparation, telling the reader what is going to be important about the book's protagonist. Read in this way, the whole of vv. 1–34 constitutes an unsettling collection of promises, threats, and paradoxes, suggesting that whoever Jesus is, he is not to be understood in conventional or common-sense terms. Thus, in relation to the book as a whole, vv. 19–34 belong more closely with what precedes than with what follows them.

In the second place, while there is a stylistic distinction between the riddling style that dominates vv. 1–18 and the more narrative style of vv. 19–34, it is by no means absolute. Interspersed in the former section, we find materials whose style and content connects them to the latter section (vv. 6–8, 15, dealing with the earthly testimony of the Baptist). Conversely, the testimony of the Baptist which dominates the second section is sometimes framed in the riddling style of the first, especially when speaking of the priority of Jesus (v. 30). If the basic difference in styles arises from John's use of an existing hymn as the basis for vv. 1–18, the result of the redaction process which has brought the hymn into its present relation to the Gospel has been to blur the distinction by interlacing it with the prose materials about John the Baptist. We might well speak here of a double prologue, heavenly and earthly, the one part dealing with the preexistence and incarnation of the logos, the other with his introduction to an earthly audience ill-equipped to comprehend who he is.

As a contribution to the task of introducing Jesus, the opening verse of the Gospel may seem less than helpful. It is a riddling statement about a remote being who both is and is not God:

(1:1) At first, there was the logos, and the logos was with God, and the logos was God.

This introduction is extraordinarily dense. The opening words (which one might also translate "In the beginning . . .") allude to the opening words of Genesis, thus establishing that the background of all that will be said in this book is the religion of Israel. The God spoken of here is the God of Israel and the creator of this universe. The logos associated with this God is less easily identified. I have left the Greek word "logos" untranslated because it is effectively impossible to represent it in English. It may be translated "word," "saying," "speech," "reason," "plan," and so on. Given the allusion to Genesis 1, some early readers will have heard here another reference to the creation chapter, this time to God's mode of creation by speaking (e.g., "Let there be light"). They may also have heard echoes of Stoic teaching, which saw the logos as forming the link between ultimate divine will, the tangible universe, and the human mind.[3]

Yet another possible area of reference would be the Jewish wisdom traditions of John's day and earlier. Here the term might allude to a figure more commonly known as sophia (wisdom). In fact, John's way of speaking about logos bears a striking resemblance to language used about sophia in Wisdom of Solomon 7—9. There, too, we find paradoxical language which speaks of sophia sometimes as distinct from, sometimes as virtually identical with God; and we find, equally, the idea that sophia was the mediator of creation, as the logos is in John 1:3. John was not the only early Christian writer to borrow such themes for purposes of explaining who Jesus was and is. Other writers coming out of the Greek-speaking Jewish-Christian tradition also invoke them. The treatment of the "son" in Hebrews 1 is a noteworthy example; the hymnic material in Phil. 2:5–11 is at least arguably another, and one might also instance the reuse of wisdom traditions in Matthew and Luke.[4]

From John's brief reference to the theme in 1:1, it is impossible to specify exactly what he expected to cross the reader's mind in connection with the word "logos." Fortunately, he is quite clear in stressing what he himself finds important in the matter: the logos both is and is not God. The logos stands in the divine, uncreated realm as over against this cosmos; yet, the divinity of the logos is not merely to be identified with that of the absolutely unoriginate one, here called simply "God" and later on often "father." "The logos was with God," on the one hand; "the logos was God," on the other.

What results is a paradox of simultaneous unity and distinction. Later on, John will make use of it as a model for the discussion of mystical union. For the moment, however, he is content to have registered the point without enlarging on it, and he moves on at once to a related matter:

(1:2) This one was at first with God. (3) All things came to be through him, and apart from him not one thing that happened came to be.[5]

It is clear enough what is being emphasized here: the logos is the only link there is, or ever has been, between God and the created order to which the reader belongs. The logos antedates creation and can even be said to stand on God's side of the line that distinguishes the divine from the created order. The logos was also the sole agent of creation: "all things . . . through him, and apart from him, not one thing. . . ." The almost tedious fullness of expression restates one idea in such a way as to exclude all exceptions: the logos is the only link between God and God's creation.

The following verses apply this general principle more specifically to the human situation:

(1:4) In him there was life, and the life was the light of human beings. (5) And the light is shining in the dark, and the dark has not apprehended it.

As the logos is indissolubly related to God, so human beings are indissolubly related to the logos, since our life is resident only in him. What is more, this life is also light, not only our being but the understanding of that being. A motif is thus adumbrated that will be clarified only in chapters 8—11: only in turning to the logos can one come into one's own reality. To have light is also to have life; and both come from the same source.

Because this light has its ultimate source in God, it cannot cease shining, even in the dark—that is, in the context of everything that is not of God. This "everything" is, in a sense, nothing at all, for we already know that nothing has come into being except by God's working through the logos. How, then, can John even speak of "the dark" (or, at other times, "the cosmos") as if it had some independent will opposed to or different from the light? Our author makes no effort to reconcile these two kinds of sayings: on the one hand, it is his axiom that all is from God through the logos; on the other, he calls our attention to a deep division within the reality we know in day-to-day existence. However bright and constant the light, there is that within and around us that has not "apprehended" it. That is, we have neither understood it nor got the better of it.

"Apprehended" (*katelaben*) is a deliberate ambiguity. Whether we take it as meaning "comprehended, understood" or as "seized, overcame," it suggests a radical, even a world-altering transformation of our actual experience. If the dark could overcome the light, the creation would be extinguished altogether, for the light is identical with life and both are resident in the sole agent of creation. If, on the other hand, the dark once understood the light and accepted it, the darkness as such would come to an end. There would be all light and only light and ourselves immersed totally in it. Why these tensions and polarities exist in the world as we know it, John does not explain—and perhaps does not care. But that they exist is a fundamental postulate of the whole Gospel.

The prologue now shifts focus drastically, moving from ultimate realities to a historical person, John the Baptist:

(1:6) A human being came, sent from God, named John. (7) This one came for testimony, to testify about the light, so that all people might believe through him. (8) That one was not the light—but to testify about the light.

The insistence in v. 8 (to be repeated later) that John the Baptist
is not the really important figure in the story perhaps had roots
in some conflict between the Johannine community and a group
which regarded the Baptist as a primary religious authority.[6] Yet,
it also has theological importance within the Gospel: in contrast
to the logos, who is in some sense God, John the Baptist is purely
a human being and cannot do or be what only the logos can. Still,
he has a positive function: he was sent by God to give testimony
about the light so that people might believe. This is very like
what our author will say of his own purpose in writing in 20:31:
"These things have been written so that you may believe. . . ."
Since the dark has not apprehended the light on its own, it requires help—help that is human and can testify in a human way,
but is also empowered or authorized by God. For only what is of
the light can testify about the light.

The testimony of John the Baptist had a peculiarly historical
character to it in that it opened the way to a unique appearance
of the light within the human story. Therefore, the Baptist's
words point forward toward another yet to come, just as those of
our author would later point backward toward one already
departed:

(1:9) There was the real light that lights every human being coming
into the cosmos.

It is ambiguous here whether "coming" refers to "the light" or
to "every human being." The former interpretation, however,
leads on more naturally to what follows. Our author speaks here
of a new and strange mode of the logos's presence. This logos,
life, or light, which is inescapably present with us by the mere
fact that we exist only through his agency, will now enter the
created order in a new and unpredictable fashion:

(1:10) He was in the cosmos (and the cosmos had come to be through
him), and the cosmos did not know him. (11) He came to his own
place, and those who are his own did not receive him. (12) But as
many as did accept him, he gave them the right to become God's
children—those believing in his name, (13) who were born not from
flows of blood nor from will of flesh nor from a husband's will but
from God.

The unexplained conflict within the created order grows
sharper as a result of this new intrusion of the divine logos. Everything is through the logos, yet the cosmos is so deeply divided

within itself that it did not know its own maker. Only some few recognized him when he appeared. And how is one to explain them? They constitute a group defined by the gifts they have received from God. Not the gifts of the original creation, mediated through ordinary human birth, for these belong to all alike. To be conceived in a human womb (that is, constituted by the flows of menstrual blood now diverted to the uses of the pregnancy) as a result of sexual intercourse (will of the flesh) and social convention (a householder's desire for children to confirm his status in the world)—all this is to participate in the original creation and be one of "those who are his own." But to know him requires something more—to be born of God in a new sense that will become apparent only as the Gospel unfolds.

John moves only gradually toward his goal (he has yet to mention the name "Jesus"). But he speaks next of a temporary residence among us, of a becoming-flesh, so that a particular human being turned out to be transparent to the full reality of the logos. This reality was "glory" by reason of its relation to the divine; that is, it embodies the beauty, wisdom, and power of God. In relation to us, it appears as "grace" (that is, "gift"), because everything flows to us from God freely through the logos, and as "truth" (that is, in Johannine usage, "ultimate reality"), because everything we are is determined ultimately by this relationship. The person who is born from God or sent from God (like John the Baptist) can perceive this grace and truth, but can express it only in a riddling way, as in the Baptist's "after" and "before" and "prior to." In this dark language are veiled the realities of which John has already spoken only a little more plainly in v. 1:

(1:14) And the logos became flesh and tented among us; and we observed his glory—glory as of an only child from a father, full of grace and truth. (15) John testifies about him and has called out saying, "This was the one of whom I said, 'The one coming after me has come to be before me because he was prior to me.'"

The arrival of the logos in this new way is a confirmation of what was always true, but also constitutes a new era in our relationship with the creator:

(1:16) For from his fullness we have all accepted, even grace on grace. (17) For the law was given through Moses; the grace and the truth came to be through Jesus Christ. (18) As for God, no one has ever seen him; the only-child God, the one who is in the father's bosom, that one has explained.

The arrival of the logos as enfleshed in Jesus offers a kind of direct access to the fonts of reality—not some new reality, but the oldest and most fundamental one possible. It is not like Moses and Torah, for Moses only handed that on and had nothing to do with its creation. Jesus was, however wildly improbable such a claim must seem, the actual creative agent by whom everything, the reader included, exists. Beyond him stands only God; and there is no access to God except through the logos.

We have, then, as the first part of the prologue concludes, this picture before us: Jesus as one who stands on both the uncreated and the created sides of reality. As logos, he is so close to God as to be called God; yet, he is not simply identified with God, for he is "with God," "in the father's bosom." As flesh, he is the historical person Jesus. And since "no one has ever seen" God, only this now-incarnate logos can make a real difference in the human relationship with God.

The prologue continues now in a somewhat more prosaic and earthly way. The logos has now been brought down into history; accordingly, our author must clarify his exact place in the history of his time, particularly his relationship to John the Baptist, generally acknowledged among early Christians to have been a predecessor in some sense. The extensive space allotted here to the Baptist's testimony, even if it was prompted in part by actual social tensions with his followers, is a way of restating the identity of Jesus in a way appropriate to his now hidden, fleshly existence. We begin by establishing the identity of John himself as something to be understood not in terms of Israel's past, but in relation to the one coming after him:

(1:19) And this is John's testimony, when the Jews from Jerusalem sent priests and Levites to him to ask him, "You, who are you?" (20) And he admitted and did not deny and admitted, "I am not the anointed." (21) And they asked him, "What are you, then? Are you Elijah?" And he says, "I am not." "Are you the prophet?" And he answered, "No." (22) So they said to him, "Who are you? So that we can give an answer to the people that sent us. What do you say about yourself?" (23) He said, "I am 'the voice of a person calling in the wasteland, "Straighten the Lord's road,"' just as Isaiah the prophet said." (24) And they had been sent from the Pharisees. (25) And they asked him and said to him, "Why then are you baptizing, if you are not the anointed nor Elijah nor the prophet?" (26) John answered them saying, "I am baptizing with water. Right among you is standing one whom you do not know, (27) the one coming after me, the thong of whose sandal I'm not worthy to untie." (28)

These things happened in Bethany beyond the Jordan, where John was baptizing.

In a way typical of this Gospel, the Jewish authorities are here called simply "the Jews." It is an odd usage for the time and calls for a moment's reflection. Undoubtedly it arises, in some way, from the political experience of the Johannine community. Insofar as we can reconstruct their history, it appears that they were being pushed out of the larger Jewish community of which they had been a part, perhaps partly in an attack on their belief in Jesus. Who was responsible for this struggle we do not know, though it is possible that they were Palestinians, for the term I am translating "Jews" also means "Judeans," and "Judea" was the contemporary name for the whole Roman province covering Palestine. It is now generally accepted that the Johannine Christians were themselves largely Jewish; but as they were rejected by their coreligionists, they necessarily developed new ways of identifying their own group in contradistinction to the larger group that was evicting them.[7]

Unfortunately, this linguistic usage, understandable enough in its beginnings, has had disastrous consequences in later centuries by reason of its use to justify Christian anti-Judaism. Of all New Testament writings, John's Gospel has served supremely well to provide a language that would justify the plundering and murdering of Jesus' (and the author's) own people. The fault can scarcely be laid at John's own door. He could scarcely have foreseen that in a few centuries his own disenfranchised minority group would have become large and powerful enough to inflict great suffering on his own nation—much less that it would so forget his own and Jesus' teaching on love that it would choose to do so. It is incumbent on modern Christians not to use this language at all except where they must do so in dealing with historical texts, and even then we must always take care to explain that it cannot justify attacks on any modern community.

To return to the passage in hand, the major import of it seems at first to be entirely negative; it is a long list of what the Baptist is not: not the anointed (the Christ) nor any other nameable figure in the history of salvation such as Elijah returned from the court of God (Mal. 4:5–6) or the "prophet like Moses" (Deut. 18:15, 18). Isaiah, to be sure, had spoken of John's mission; but in such a way that we can understand him not at all in relation to the past—

only in relation to the one coming after him. This future figure is indeed already present, but without being recognized (cf. 1:11).

Just as in the "heavenly" prologue we heard a great deal about Jesus before he was actually named, so in the "earthly" prologue we move only gradually toward an identification of him:

(1:29) The next day, he sees Jesus coming toward him and says, "See! The lamb of God that takes away the sin of the cosmos. (30) This is the one about whom I said, 'After me is coming a man who has come to be before me because he was prior to me.' (31) And *I* did not know him; but so that he might be revealed to Israel, for this reason *I* came baptizing in water." (32) And John testified, saying, "I have watched the spirit descending as a dove from heaven, and it stayed on him. (33) And *I* did not know him; but the one who had sent me to baptize in water, that one said to me, 'On whomever you see the spirit descending and staying on him, this is the one who baptizes in holy spirit.' (34) And I have seen it, and I have given my testimony that this is the son of God."

Here, John the Baptist is the means for conveying several important pieces of information about Jesus, all reinforcing what we have already learned. Just as in the creation, the logos was the only link between creator and cosmos, so, too, the logos made flesh is the one means of reconciliation between the two now that they are estranged. John's baptism is merely preparatory. Jesus is the lamb that takes away sin (a sacrificial image not important elsewhere in the Gospel); he is also the bearer of the spirit. This spirit he will later hand on to the disciples, giving them, too, the power to undo sin (20:22). Thus, Jesus is not only the original link between God and cosmos, but also the agent of reconciliation who alone will overcome the estrangement between dark and light, between humanity and God.

In this way, a preliminary statement of the theological situation presupposed by our author lies before us. To restate it in terms focused now on the reader of the work: you are totally dependent on God through the logos, having no being of any kind except through him. At the same time, you participate in the present reality of estrangement, the darkness which cannot cope with the light, either to understand or to overcome it, the cosmos which does not know or accept its own maker. To overcome this estrangement, there is recourse to one being only, the same logos through whom we first came to be; this logos is now enfleshed in Jesus, who takes away sin, baptizes in holy spirit, and thus grants the right to become children of God in a new sense.

2
CONVERSION
(John 1:35—2:25)

How does the new relationship with God, made possible in Jesus, become actual for the individual? Our author says that he wrote the Gospel "so that you may believe that Jesus is the anointed, the son of God, and so that, as you believe, you might have life in his name" (20:31). Our author repeatedly emphasizes this point; the verb "to believe" (*pisteuō*) is one of the most common words in the book. Yet, it is difficult to unravel what it means for John. When we first encounter it in the narratives to follow, it seems to mean little more than conversion, the first faith-recognition that Jesus is significant for one's life. As such, it is weak and fallible and even, at moments, comic.

Again, we begin rather gradually:

(1:35) The next day again John was standing there—and two of his disciples—(36) and after watching Jesus as he walked around, he says, "See! The lamb of God." (37) And the two disciples heard him talking and followed Jesus. (38) But Jesus, when he had turned round and observed them following him, says to them, "What do you want?" And they said to him, "Rabbi (which means "Teacher" in translation), where are you staying?" (39) He says to them, "Come, and you'll see." So they came and saw where he was staying; and they stayed with him that day. It was about four o'clock. (40) Andrew, Simon Peter's brother, was one of the pair that had heard what John said and followed him. (41) This one first finds his own brother Simon and says to him, "We have found the messiah (which is translated "anointed")." (42) He brought him to Jesus. Jesus, after looking at him, said, "You are Simon, son of John; you shall be called Cephas (which is translated "Peter/Rock")."

These first conversions are almost incidental in nature. John the

21

Baptist may not have been talking to anyone in particular; indeed, the language rather suggests that the two disciples had merely overheard him. They approach Jesus anonymously, and with no particular notion what to expect. The expression "lamb of God" could have had no clear meaning for them; and when Jesus asks them what they want, they have no real answer. At most, they want, in their curiosity, to see more of Jesus—and he allows them that. For one of them, the day proves decisive, and he goes at once, though it is now supper time, and brings his brother. What has happened to the other? There is no indication, and we are free to think that he found the whole day a bore and an imposition. There is nothing automatic about conversion.[1]

It may seem that Andrew's conversion is all that one could ask. From the very beginning, he makes a correct confession of Jesus; he is indeed the anointed, as John has already said in the prologue (1:17). He at once begins the disciple's work of bringing others (cf. 17:20), and his first convert is so impressive that Jesus surnames him "Rock." John expects the reader to know who Simon is even before he is introduced in the narrative—another confirmation of the man's importance. Yet, this is not all there is to be said about conversion:

(1:43) The next day, he wanted to go off into Galilee. And he finds Philip, and Jesus says to him, "Follow me." (44) (Philip was from Bethsaida, from the city of Andrew and Peter.) (45) Philip finds Nathanael and says to him, "We've found the one Moses wrote about in the Law—the prophets, too—Jesus son of Joseph, the one from Nazareth." (46) And Nathanael said to him, "Can there be anything good from *Nazareth?*" Philip says to him, "Come and see!" (47) Jesus saw Nathanael coming toward him and says of him, "See! One who is really an Israelite; there is no deceit in him!" (48) Nathanael says to him, "Where do you know me from?" Jesus answered and said to him, "Before Philip called you, while you were under the fig tree, I saw you." (49) Nathanael answered him, "Rabbi, you are the son of God; you are king of Israel." (50) Jesus answered and said to him, "Because I told you that I had seen you under the fig tree, do you believe?! You will see greater things than these!" (51) And he says to him, "Amen, amen, I say to you all: You shall see heaven opened up and the angels of God climbing up and down on the son of humanity."

This narrative begins in a plausible way, with Jesus' calling of Philip. Since Philip is described as a fellow townsman of Andrew and Peter, we readily assume that he knows all the news of the previous day. He participates in the enthusiasm of those who became disciples before him and goes off to call his own friend Nathanael. But now things go a little awry. Nathanael is a snob. Though he was himself from Cana (21:2), near Nazareth, he has adopted the prevalent view that Galilean religion was inferior to that of Judea. So confident is he of his credentials that when Jesus compliments him, he accepts the accolade without demur and only wonders where Jesus has had the privilege of knowing him. He has not, of course, been to Jesus' village in Upper Galilee himself. When Jesus replies, however, telling him where he was before Philip called him, he is taken completely aback. Why?

What follows can only be understood on the assumption that Nathanael believes he has witnessed a miracle. But what sort of miracle? Not anything impressive—an exorcism (there are none in this Gospel), a healing, a raising of the dead—only a rather minor bit of second sight, a prophetic gift, to be sure (one may think of the finding of the lost asses in 1 Samuel 9), but hardly an impressive miracle. Like Andrew earlier, Nathanael confesses Jesus in terms unimpeachably correct. Jesus is, as John the Baptist has already said, "son of God"; he is "king of Israel"—equivalent to Andrew's confession of him as "anointed." The joke, however, lies in seeing Nathanael's urbanity suddenly deflated by something so minor, so that his original scorn turns into this extravagant (if true) confession without further ado.

Jesus, accordingly, makes fun of him. One might paraphrase his response thus: "Do you really believe for so trivial a reason? I could give you better reasons than that; perhaps you have come too cheap." Yet, when Jesus goes on to tell the disciples what "greater things" they will see, he describes something which will not in fact happen anywhere in this Gospel—a vision of a human being, presumably himself, serving as Jacob's ladder (cf. Gen. 28:10–12). The odd phrase that he uses—"son of humanity"—stands as a counterweight to Nathanael's "son of God," not because Nathanael was wrong theologically but because he spoke for the wrong reasons and without knowing what he said. He spoke out of admiration for a miracle, with no sense of Jesus' real humanity. Now Jesus calls attention to that humanity and, in the process, explains the true meaning of the phrase "son of God": Jesus is the ladder, the only link, connecting heaven and earth; even the angels of God must come and go by way of him. To see this (with the eye of the spirit, to be sure) would be good grounds for believing.[2]

All this is not to say that Nathanael's conversion is wrong. He will reappear in the Appendix (21:2), suggesting that the Johannine community had a tradition of him as a faithful disciple. His conversion is only comical and, as such, it is a model of all conversions. It is a lucky stab in the dark, not an act of knowledge and understanding. Perhaps, if the convert perseveres, it will become the basis for something more. In the meantime, however, our author places next to Nathanael the model of a different and deeper approach to Jesus, summed up in Jesus' mother:[3]

(2:1) And on the third day a wedding took place in Cana of Galilee, and the mother of Jesus was there. (2) And Jesus, too, was invited to the wedding, along with his disciples. (3) And when the wine had run out, the mother of Jesus says to him, "They have no wine." (4) Jesus says to her, "What do you have to do with me, lady? My hour is not yet here." (5) His mother says to the servants, "Anything at all that he tells you, do." (6) Now, there were six stone water jars standing there for the Jews' purification rites, holding twenty to twenty-five gallons each.[4] (7) Jesus says to them, "Fill the jars with water." And they filled them to the brim. (8) And he says to them, "Ladle some out now and take it to the master of the banquet." And they took it. (9) Now, when the master of the banquet tasted the water now become wine and did not know where it was from (though the servants knew who had ladled the water out), the master of the banquet calls the bridegroom (10) and says to him, "Everybody serves the good wine first—and the poorer stuff when people are drunk. You've kept the good wine till now!" (11) This beginning of the signs Jesus did in Cana of Galilee and revealed his glory; and his disciples believed in him.

There are two aspects of this narrative equally important in the context: one is the interaction between Jesus and his mother which sets the stage for the miracle; the other is John's designation of the miracle as a "sign," which suggests something of how we are to interpret its meaning in this Gospel.

The conversation between Jesus and Mary is difficult and does not yield easily to interpretation. Knowing about the shortage of provisions, she merely reports to him, "They have no wine." Yet, he understands this as in some way a claim on him and rejects it. The expression "What do you have to do with me?" means as little in Greek as in English. Early Christians, however, were familiar with it in their Greek Bible as translation of a Hebrew phrase; and one finds it elsewhere in the New Testament also (e.g., in Mark 5:7 where the possessed man addresses this same question to Jesus). If one seeks a functional equivalent to it in

English it would perhaps be something on the order of "stay out of my business."[5]

Jesus thus rejects the unspoken request and reinforces his refusal with another difficult phrase: "My hour is not yet here." Elsewhere in John's Gospel, such language about Jesus' "hour" refers to the time of his passion and death (7:30; 8:20) or, as it is expressed in 13:1, of his crossing over from the cosmos to the father. Does it mean that here? That does not seem quite appropriate, for this miracle does not in fact get Jesus into any trouble or lead in any way toward the passion. Perhaps we may attribute to the phrase a larger meaning which will embrace both this and the later instances of its use: Jesus' "hour" is the whole large work of bringing cosmos and creator back together and the plan which guides that work. Providing wine at a marriage banquet in Cana is not part of that plan.

Since Jesus has now refused to become involved in the matter, should this not end the story? Instead, Mary turns to the servants and gives them interesting instructions: "Anything at all that he tells you, do." John has combined two indefinite relative constructions in Greek (*ho ti* and *ho an*), either of which by itself would mean "whatever." Combining the two, he creates a kind of double vagueness—not quite so uncertain as a conditional form (if he should tell you anything, do it) but very near it. Mary's persistence wins the day, for Jesus does go on to give the servants instructions which set the miracle in train.

But what is the significance of Mary's role here? One could see her as impertinent; yet, she is a key agent in bringing about "this beginning of the signs." Accordingly, John must take her role as a positive one; and we can see two aspects of her behavior that suggest how this might be. The first lies in the contrast she makes with Nathanael in the preceding story. Nathanael is scornful until a minor miracle, hardly a miracle at all, spins him completely around and makes a believer of him. Mary, on the other hand, who has presumably seen no signs (this being the first), requires none, but believes beforehand that Jesus can do anything necessary and desirable.[6] This brings us to the second way in which Mary is a positive example: the substance of her belief, as manifested in her actions, is in full accord with the theology laid out in the prologue. Acknowledging Jesus as the only link between God and the creation, she turns to him at once in a time of need (albeit a purely day-to-day need, not directly related to Jesus' mission); and, when rebuffed, she does not turn elsewhere, for there is nowhere else to turn. She waits to see what the only source of good will in fact do: "Anything at all that he tells you, do." She is a model, then, of right believing in contrast to the shallow inadequacy of most conversions. (The latter point will be reaffirmed in 2:23–25.)

Mary's believing is not dependent on signs, but John suggests that it is normal for signs to play a role in connection with conversion and with the confirmation of belief. On one level, then, "sign" means "miracle" here—a worthier example of the kind of thing that prompted Nathanael to believe. Yet it is also much more. For John, the ability to perform miracles was not what made Jesus important. He has already ascribed to the logos a glory far greater than that of any miracle worker—"glory as of an only child from a father" (1:14). Now he tells us that Jesus "revealed his glory" through the sign, meaning that the same note of unique access to God is again struck here.

Jesus' glory, moreover, is "full of grace and truth" (1:14), qualities that came into being through Jesus and are contrasted to the Law that was given through Moses (1:17). John underlines this contrast in the present narrative by the way he recounts the story. He emphasizes the large water jars and their ritual function, which is of the Law. Equally, he emphasizes the unexpectedness of the transformed water, which is not only wine now but (to the confusion of the banquet master's etiquette) the best of wine. Here is a real grace, but a hidden one, in conformity with John's earlier claim that only a few actually receive the logos at his coming (1:10–13). In all this, we observe that Jesus discards the "legal" function of purification in order to save a bridal banquet— which will become an image of his own ministry in chapter 3.

The deed, then, is indeed a sign of Jesus' authority—not only of the ability to work miracles, but of the ultimate, creative authority of the logos who substitutes grace and truth for the Law. The following narrative reiterates the point in a new and more explicit way:

> (2:12) After this, he went down to Capernaum—he and his mother and brothers and his disciples; and he stayed[7] there not many days. (13) And the Jews' passover was near, and Jesus went up to Jerusalem. (14) And he found in the temple the people who sold cattle and sheep and pigeons and the money-changers at their seats. (15) And he made a whip of cords and ran them all out of the temple, sheep and cattle

alike, and dumped out the money-changers' coins and overturned their tables; (16) and to the people selling pigeons he said, "Get these things out of here; don't make my father's house a marketplace." (17) His disciples remembered that it was in writing: "Jealousy for your house will devour me." (18) The Jews, then, responded and said to him, "What sign do you show us—that you do these things!" (19) Jesus answered and said to them, "Tear this temple down, and in three days I will raise it." (20) So the Jews said, "This temple has taken forty-six years to build, and you're going to raise it in three days?" (21) But that one was talking about the temple of his body. (22) So when he was raised from the dead, his disciples remembered his saying this; and they believed the writing and the word that Jesus spoke.

The main theme of this narrative is the same as that of the Cana miracle: replacement of the old religion with the new reality of Jesus' presence. As purification yields to the banquet of wine, so the old temple with its sacrifices gives way to Jesus' own person as the means of access to God. John's peculiar placement of this episode (the other three Gospels all place it, with more probability, as a prelude to the passion) brings out this message.[8] Jesus, to be sure, treats the Jerusalem temple with a certain respect when he clears it of all mundane activities. Yet, he is also disrupting the whole process of procuring and offering sacrifices and gifts—that is, the traffic between earth and heaven that is prescribed in the Law. In its place, though no one as yet understands, he sets himself.

This passage, then, functions primarily to reiterate the theology first introduced in the prologue. Yet, the theme of conversion has not been abandoned. For one thing, we have a picture of Jesus' family and disciples moving to Capernaum together (though Jesus does not stay there long), thus suggesting that his family has now rallied to him.[9] The inadequacy of his brothers' conversion, however, will become apparent in due course. For another thing, Jesus' disciples are shown still to have only incomplete understanding. Although they have been converted and have been said to "believe" after the first sign at Cana, we are now told that there were aspects of belief to which they would attain only after Jesus' resurrection. Conversion is only a beginning.

It is not, moreover, a very trustworthy beginning:

(2:23) Now, while he was at Jerusalem at the passover at the feast, many people believed in his name, seeing his signs that he was doing. (24) But Jesus himself did not trust himself to them because he knew all people (25) and because he had no need for anyone to tell him about humanity. For he himself knew what was in humanity.

This summary passage brings the discussion of conversion to a close on a pessimistic note. There are many who believe (*pisteuō*) because they see signs; but Jesus knows better than to trust (same Greek verb, *pisteuō*) himself to them. Conversion is easy for human beings, but it does not mean much by itself. It does not free us from the fickleness or treachery that are features of our humanity. There is yet further to go in becoming a child of God.

3
BAPTISM
(John 3:1—5:47)

For Christians, the normal sequel to conversion was and is baptism. For the earliest believers, who were Jewish, there was presumably no prolonged catechesis, since there was only one new teaching for them to learn—that Jesus is Messiah. The disciples, in this Gospel, have already learned that (1:41). The question, then, is what exactly is baptism for our author? What does it mean? What does it accomplish? These questions shape the materials of this section of the Gospel. A note on the translation of the following sections: there is a play here on the Greek word *pneuma*, variously equivalent in English to "wind," "breath," and "spirit." Since the play on words is impossible to duplicate in English, I have arbitrarily used the translation "wind" throughout. It is the same Greek word, however, that is translated "spirit" elsewhere in this work.

(3:1) There was a person from the Pharisees, named Nicodemus, a member of the Jewish high council. (2) This one came to him at night and said to him, "Rabbi, we know that you've come from God as teacher, for no one can do these signs that you're doing unless God is with him." (3) Jesus replied and said to him, "Amen, amen, I say to you, unless one gets born again [or, from above], one cannot see the reign of God." (4) Nicodemus says to him, "How can a person get born when he's old? Can he enter his mother's womb a second time and be born?" (5) Jesus replied, "Amen, amen, I say to you, unless one is born of water and wind, one cannot enter the reign of God. (6) What is born of the flesh is flesh, and what is born of the wind is wind. (7) Don't be surprised that I've told you, 'You all have to be born again [or, from above].' (8) The wind blows where it likes, and you hear its sound, but you don't know where it's coming from and where it's going. That's how it is with everyone that's born of the wind."

29

Nicodemus is an important figure—a member of the Sanhedrin, the supreme Jewish religious-legal-political organ under the Roman government; and yet, he comes to Jesus as a convert of a sort. His confession falls short of some previously made (that Jesus is Messiah, son of God, king of Israel); but it is not untrue, from John's point of view. Jesus is, indeed, a teacher from God;[1] and it is an act of humility and of daring for Nicodemus, himself a teacher of official standing, to come and acknowledge him. Yet, he comes "at night"—a phrase which recalls "the dark" that cannot apprehend the logos. This represents John's judgment on all conversion as such. While it may be a step in the right direction, conversion does not, of itself, bring a person out of the dark into the light.

Accordingly, John has Jesus at once shift the ground of the discussion. He replies to Nicodemus's confession with a non sequitur, an "inappropriate response," which moves us to the next stage of Christian experience—baptismal rebirth. Yet, he introduces the subject in an obscure and allusive way. The goal of faith is to see or even enter the reign of God, that is, to experience God's salvation as direct and immediate rule over the cosmos. The prologue has already told us that the cosmos has come to be in opposition to its creator and to the creator's logos. The reign of God will overcome that opposition and restore the original richness and concord of the relationship. Such is the life to which rebirth is the gateway.

The early Christians had a variety of ways of describing Baptism and its meaning: in the Pauline churches, one spoke of it as an experience of death and resurrection (Rom. 6:3–10; Col. 2:12); others used the analogy of washing (e.g., 1 Peter 3:21; Heb. 10:22). John here uses the image of birth, the baptismal water being seen as analogous to the amniotic fluid. At first, however, he introduces the theme with an ambiguous phrase "to be born *anōthen*." The Greek term can equally well mean "again" or "from above"; here, it probably means both at once. The prologue spoke of those who are born "not from flows of blood nor from will of flesh nor from a husband's will but from God" (1:13). To be born from God and to be born "from above" would seem to come to much the same thing.

Nicodemus, however, understands Jesus to mean "born again." And that is right, too. This is another kind of birth—not of flesh, but of water and wind. The water in question is the external sign of Baptism, the wind/spirit its inner reality; for John distinguishes between the two just as 1 Peter and Hebrews do in the passages noted above. It is not the washing with or dipping in water that affects the reality of the baptized person, but an inner, spiritual alteration held to be the accompaniment of the rite.[2]

One is not to overestimate the value of this rite, however; it is no ultimate truth.

> (3:9) Nicodemus replied and said to him, "How can these things happen?" (10) Jesus answered and said to him, "Are *you* Israel's teacher and you don't know these things? (11) Amen, amen, I say to you that we tell what we know and we testify to what we have seen—and you people don't accept our testimony. (12) If I've told you the earthly things and you don't believe, how will you believe if I tell you the heavenly things? (13) And no one has gone up into heaven except that one who came down from heaven, the son of humanity. (14) And just as Moses lifted up the serpent in the wasteland, so the son of humanity has to be lifted up, (15) so that everybody that believes in him may have everlasting life."

Jesus' teaching about birth from water and wind may seem difficult (though presumably the Christian reader has an advantage here over Nicodemus). Yet, these are only "the earthly things." There are other, heavenly things yet to come. And none of these things, earthly or heavenly, will be credible except on the presupposition that Jesus is uniquely qualified to speak of them. Once again, he is the only link between God and the creation. In saying that no one has ascended to heaven, John has Jesus deny a widely held ancient belief in the possibility of celestial journeys; compare Paul's claim to have made such an ascent in 2 Cor. 12:1–5. There is only the son of humanity who has come down from heaven—and will be "lifted up" on his return thither. (In these words, Jesus first hints that the cross will be the way of his return.)

The purpose of Jesus' descent and ascent is to make everlasting life[3] available to those who believe—a point expanded upon in the following passage. It is difficult to say whether Jesus is still speaking or John has taken over in his own voice; I assume the latter in my translation.

> (3:16) For God loved the cosmos so much that he gave his only son, so that everybody who believes in him would not be destroyed but would have everlasting life. (17) For God did not send the son into the cosmos to judge the cosmos, but for the cosmos to be saved through him. (18) The one who believes in him is not brought to judgment; the one who does not believe has already been judged

because he has not believed in the name of God's only son. (19) And this is the judgment—that the light has come into the cosmos and people have loved the dark more than the light, for their acts were evil. (20) For everyone who does bad things hates the light and does not come to the light, so that his actions will not be exposed. (21) But the one who does the truth comes to the light, so that his actions will be revealed as having been accomplished in God.

The creation is beloved of the creator. However much it may have become estranged, it is not God's objective to take vengeance on it; rather to call it back into that right relationship which is true and everlasting life. After all, life is "in" the logos and is identical with light (1:4). To be deprived of God is to be deprived of our own existence. Yet, the estrangement is real and is not to be overcome by divine fiat. The sending of the son does not force salvation on anyone, but makes it possible for those who, for whatever mysterious reasons, are or become doers of the truth. Nicodemus has come to Jesus, who is the light; but he has come "at night." The ambiguity of his situation is not unique to him, but describes the human situation as such.

Since Jesus has now asserted the necessity of baptism as the next step toward the reign of God or everlasting life—that is, toward true created existence, it is appropriate that he himself should make this baptism available. No other Gospel ascribes to Jesus the following activity:

(3:22) After these things, Jesus went—and his disciples—into the Judean countryside, and he spent time with them there and was baptizing. (23) And John, too, was baptizing at Aenon near Saleim, because there were many streams there; and people were coming and getting baptized. (24) For John had not yet been thrown into prison. (25) So an argument arose on the part of John's disciples with a Jew; the subject was purification. (26) And they came to John and said to him, "Rabbi, the man who was with you in the trans-Jordan, the one you testified to—see, this man is baptizing and all the people are going to him." (27) John replied and said, "A person cannot get anything at all unless it's been given him from heaven. (28) You yourselves bear me witness that I said, '*I'm* not the anointed,' rather 'I've been sent before that one.' (29) The man who has the bride is the bridegroom; but the bridegroom's friend, who stands and listens to him, is very glad at the bridegroom's voice. This joy of mine, then, is full. (30) That one has to grow, and I have to decline."

This short narrative seems a bit clumsy in the way the subject of Jesus is raised for John the Baptist. Exactly what was the argument about purification? Why did Jesus' name come into it?

On the whole, a capable narrator prefers not to leave such un-answered questions dangling in the air to distract the reader. The clue to this passage, however, must surely lie in the earlier one where the themes of purification and wedding were brought into contact with each other—the first miracle at Cana (2:1–11). In that passage, Jesus replaced the water of purification with the wine of feasting. Here, too, purification is mentioned only to be dropped. One senses that baptism itself, though important to John, is being subtly derogated. It is not the real point, not an end in itself. God's aim is not the preparation, but the feast; accordingly, the preliminary mission given to the Baptist must now come to a halt and yield to the one who is the central figure in that feast.

The following discourse continues the theological exposition. John the Baptist may still be speaking, but it is more likely that our author interjects his own voice.

> (3:31) The one that comes from above is over all; the one from the earth is of the earth and speaks from the earth. The one coming from heaven is over all. (32) What he has seen and heard, to this he testifies, and no one accepts his testimony. (33) The one who has accepted his testimony has attested that God is true. (34) For the one that God has sent speaks God's words, for he is not stingy in giving the spirit. (35) The father loves the son and has put all things in his hand. (36) The one who believes in the son has everlasting life; but the one who disobeys the son will not see life, but God's wrath stays on him.

The previous theological discourse (3:16–21) held that judgment is connected with one's attitude toward the son, basing this on the nature of those being judged: some love the light, some the dark. The present short discourse reaffirms that the son is important not only because he serves as a touchstone of human moral qualities, but because he is the medium by which God gives this world its reality. He is "from above," "from heaven." He is fully endowed with spirit, so that he even "speaks God's words." All things are in his power. Therefore there is no avoiding the necessity to adopt some position with regard to him—which will also be a position with regard to God and to our own lives.

As John returns us to the narrative, we find that Jesus' success as a baptizer has drawn official attention to him. It is apparently unwelcome attention. He withdraws from the area near Jerusalem, and, while traveling, has a remarkable encounter with more than a touch of very serious comedy about it:

(4:1) When Jesus, then, found out that the Pharisees had heard that
Jesus was making and baptizing more disciples than John—(2)
though Jesus in fact was not baptizing them; his disciples were—(3)
he left Judea and went away again into Galilee. (4) And he had to
pass through Samaria. (5) He came then to a city of Samaria called
Sychar, near the piece of land that Jacob gave to his son Joseph. (6)
And Jacob's spring was there. Jesus, then, worn out from the traveling, took a seat just so by the spring. It was about noon.

Jesus has brought his disciples into the work of baptizing now.
It is not enough that Christians should be baptized themselves;
they also become agents in the spread of Jesus' word. (We shall
see, however, that they have something to learn in this respect.)
As they withdraw from Judea, their route takes them through
hostile country. Jews and Samaritans were closely related, but
very antagonistic to one another.

(4:7) A woman of Samaria comes to draw water.[4] Jesus says to her,
"Give me a drink"; (8) for his disciples had gone off into the city to
buy provisions. (9) So the Samaritan woman says to him, "How can
you, a Jewish man, ask a drink from me, a Samaritan woman?" (For
Jews do not share dishes with Samaritans.) (10) Jesus answered and
said to her, "If you knew God's gift and who it is that's saying to
you, 'Give me a drink,' you would ask him and he would give you
living water." (11) The woman says to him, "Sir, you don't even
have a bucket and the well is deep. Where, then, do you get the living
water? (12) Are you greater than our father Jacob, who gave us the
well and drank from it himself—and his sons and his cattle?" (13)
Jesus answered and said to her, "Everybody that drinks from this
water will get thirsty again; (14) but whoever drinks from the water
that I'll give him will never get thirsty to all eternity, but the water
that I'll give him will become in him a spring of water gushing out
into everlasting life." (15) The woman says to him, "Sir, give me
this water, so that I won't get thirsty or come out here to draw."

Jesus initiates this dialogue by breaching all dictates of etiquette: a Jewish religious teacher has no business being seen in
conversation with a lone Samaritan woman in a spot deserted at
this hour of the day. She does not seem altogether happy about
it herself and tries to brush him off. He keeps her attention, however, by hinting at a remarkable gift that is in his power to give—
living (that is, running) water.[5] As the discussion progresses, it
appears that this water is miraculous in that it permanently fore-
stalls thirst. We should expect that this water is connected with
Baptism, since John prefaced this narrative (4:1) with a reference
to that rite. The fact that it is "living" water may also echo early
Christian baptismal practice, which preferred the use of running

water.[6] There is an apparent awkwardness in that Jesus speaks
of water for drinking rather than for washing; but this, too, may
have some connection with ancient baptismal practice, which
sometimes included a drink of water along with the dipping or
washing in it.[7] Still, in the present context, there is a certain shift
of emphasis. What this woman will receive (and what will over-
flow from her onto others) is not the rite of Baptism, but Jesus'
teaching—especially his teaching about himself and his work.

The reader of the Gospel assumes at this point that Jesus is
speaking figuratively, as he did with Nicodemus or Nathanael;
but the woman cannot know this and challenges Jesus to make
good his offer: "If you knew . . . , you would ask . . ." And so she
asks. In a conversation which began with Jesus asking for a drink,
the tables are now turned and the woman asks for water. But the
gift turns on a matter of self-knowledge.

> (4:16) He says to her, "Go, call your husband, and come here." (17)
> The woman answered and said to him, "I don't have a husband."
> Jesus says to her, "You were right to say 'I don't have a husband';
> (18) for you've had five husbands and the one you have now isn't
> your husband. You spoke the truth there." (19) The woman says to
> him, "Sir, I see that you're a prophet. (20) Our ancestors worshiped
> on this mountain; and you people say that the place where one has
> to worship is in Jerusalem." (21) Jesus says to her, "Believe me, lady;
> the hour is coming when you will worship the father neither on this
> mountain nor in Jerusalem. (22) You people worship something you
> don't know; we worship what we do know, because salvation is from
> the Jews. (23) But the hour is coming—and it's here now—when the
> true worshipers will worship the father in spirit and truth, for in fact
> the father wants just such people as his worshipers. (24) God is spirit,
> and those who worship him must worship in spirit and truth." (25)
> The woman says to him, "I know messiah is coming, the one called
> 'anointed.' When that one comes, he'll explain everything to us."
> (26) Jesus says to her, "I, the one talking to you, am he."

When the woman asks for the gift, it is a kind of conversion,
a turning toward Jesus, that is no more foolish, really, than that
of Nathanael. Jesus tells her to come back with her husband. The
request is reasonable enough on the surface; if her husband is
present, Jesus avoids any appearance of illicit activity—and perhaps the husband was even necessary for contractual reasons. Yet,
it is really a ploy which enables Jesus to reveal his knowledge of
her past, knowledge which no Jewish stranger could have by normal means. It is very like the second sight which so impressed
Nathanael (1:48–49), but this woman is more cautious in her

response. She acknowledges that Jesus has prophetic powers and, very sensibly, seeks to shift the conversation from her own history to a more neutral topic—religion.

Here, too, it seems she is not quite safe. She brings out a topic endlessly argued between Samaritans and Jews: Where was the one place (Deut. 12:1–14) God had chosen to be worshiped—Gerizim or Jerusalem? She expects to settle into the familiar debate on the subject, but Jesus (albeit with a brief reaffirmation of Jewish priority) sweeps the whole matter aside: "That was then; this is now. A new order is already replacing the old and its 'place' of worship is 'in spirit and truth.'"[8] This response, in effect, removes the old religious landmarks and leaves the discussion without further criteria. The woman then seeks to dismiss the whole business: "One day—no doubt far hence—messiah will come and settle it." Jesus' identification of himself leaves her nowhere else to retreat.

One could understand well enough if she were simply to return home shaking her head over an encounter with a crazy foreigner. Yet, Jesus' prophetic utterance has at least raised questions in her mind.

> (4:27) And at this his disciples came back, and they were surprised that he was talking with a woman. Yet, no one said, "What do you want?" or "Why are you talking with her?" (28) So the woman left her water jar and went off into the city and says to the people, (29) "Come see a person who's told me everything I ever did! You don't suppose this is the anointed?" (30) They left the city and were coming toward him.

While the disciples seem upset at Jesus' breach of etiquette, they sense that they must let matters alone and they do not question either the woman or Jesus. The woman, meantime, lets her new discovery take precedence over her original errand and hurries back to share it with her neighbors. She speaks cautiously, but with effect. Little do the disciples know that her role is one of great importance and touches them intimately.

> (4:31) Meanwhile, the disciples were asking him, saying, "Rabbi, eat something." (32) But he said to them, "I have food to eat that you don't know of." (33) So the disciples were saying to each other, "Did somebody bring him something to eat?" (34) Jesus says to them, "My food is to do the will of the one who sent me and to finish his work. (35) Haven't you been saying, 'Four months yet and the harvest is coming'? Look, I tell you; raise your eyes and see how the fields are white for harvest. Already (36) the harvester is getting paid and is

gathering a crop for everlasting life, so that the sower and the har-
vester may be glad together. (37) For in this respect it's a true saying
that 'It's one person that sows and another that harvests.' (38) I've
sent you to harvest what you haven't labored over. Others have
worked hard, and you've gotten the benefit of their work."

The exchange between Jesus and his disciples about food is
perplexing, but it is analogous with the previous discussion (with
the woman) about water. Just as there is a kind of water which
cancels out all thirst, so there is a kind of food that cancels all
hunger. It is not any material, tangible food, however; and once
again our attention is directed to the inner or spiritual reality of
relationship with God. The only ultimately important thing is to
get on with God's work. The disciples, it seems, had remarked
recently that harvest was four months off. Look now, Jesus says,
at the stream of people coming from the city, and you'll see that
it is already here. The disciples will participate in this harvest,
but must recognize that it is the result of others' labor. Whose
labor, exactly? That of Jesus himself, for one.[9] But there is another, too, who has labored—the Samaritan woman who summoned the approaching crowd:

(4:39) And from that city many of the Samaritans believed in him
on account of what the woman said when she testified, "He told me
everything I ever did." (40) So when the Samaritans reached him,
they asked him to stay with them; and he stayed there two days.
(41) And many more believed on account of what he had to say. (42)
And they would say to the woman, "It's no longer because of what
you said that we believe, for we've heard, ourselves, and know that
this is really the savior of the cosmos."

The woman's testimony was persuasive enough to lead the people
of her city to invite Jesus to stay there—a highly exceptional
gesture toward a Jew. If they go on to say to her that they now
believe on the basis of Jesus' own words and not just hers, that
is not to minimize her importance, but to confirm it. She is an
evangelist, like Andrew and Philip in chapter 1, but a good deal
more effective. One result of her achievement is that Jesus now
has, it would seem, as many Samaritans who believe in him as
Jews; and it is not enough here for him to be called simply "messiah" or "anointed." Samaritans and Jews alike may have expected a messiah; they did not expect the same messiah. Thus,
his new Samaritan followers refer to him by a more general, but
deeply accurate title—"savior of the cosmos."

All this is the result of (1) Jesus' activity in baptizing and (2) a conversation with a Samaritan woman about running water. Yet, there is no reference to any baptisms in Sychar itself. Why? In terms of the narrative here, Jesus has already stopped baptizing personally (4:2); probably one is to assume that the disciples now did this work. Accordingly, there is no further reference to it because it is not part of his distinctive activity. At a deeper level, we see in this omission an emphasis on the missionary aspect of baptism. In the conversation with Nicodemus, baptism appears to be purely a matter of individual advantage; without it, one does not enter the reign of God. The living water that the Samaritan woman receives, however, is a message which extends its benefits at once to all around her—"a spring of water gushing out into everlasting life" (4:14).

From Sychar, Jesus now continues the trip into Galilee begun at 4:3:

> (4:43) But after two days, he left there for Galilee, (44) for Jesus himself testified that a prophet gets no honor in his own homeland. (45) When he came into Galilee, then, the Galileans received him, having seen everything that he did in Jerusalem at the feast—for they, too, had come to the feast.

This is a difficult passage to make sense of, for Galilee would seem to *be* Jesus' homeland; he is described as being "from Nazareth" and we meet his mother and brothers at Galilean sites. The Synoptic evangelists, moreover, record this same saying about a prophet's homeland, and all three treat it as a condemnation of the people at Nazareth. Yet, here it is Jesus' reason for going on to Galilee and not back to Judea; and the Galileans do in fact take him seriously when he arrives. What, then, is the point? The ancestral homeland (*patris*, literally "fatherland") of the tribe of Judah lay to the south of Jerusalem; from David's time, Jerusalem became their symbolic center. In his conversation with the Samaritan woman, Jesus had linked Jerusalem with the Jewish claim to special relationship with God—"salvation is of the Jews." There was therefore a special importance attached to his reception at Jerusalem, and he assumes it will continue to grow more hostile. John thus handles the saying more "theologically" than the other three evangelists. It is not a testimony to Jesus' individual problems with immediate neighbors, but reminds the reader that the prophets were often rejected by their own people when they brought God's message.

The Galileans, in any case, are not altogether faultless. They

believe because they have seen signs, and we have already been
warned how fragile such belief is (2:23–25). Jesus will, in fact,
reject it in the following story:

(4:46) He came again, then, to Cana of Galilee, where he had made
the water wine. And there was a certain royal official whose son was
sick at Capernaum. (47) When this man heard that Jesus had come
out of Judea into Galilee, he went off to meet him and asked him
to come down and heal his son, for he was about to die. (48) Jesus,
then, said to him, "Unless you people see signs and portents, you'll
never believe." (49) The royal official says to him, "Sir, come down
before my child dies." (50) Jesus says to him, "Go; your son is going
to live." The man believed what Jesus said to him and went. (51)
And as he was already on the way down, his slaves met him, saying
that his son was going to live. (52) So he enquired of them the hour
when he got better. So they told him, "Yesterday, at one in the af-
ternoon, the fever left him." (53) So the father knew that it was the
very hour when Jesus had said to him, "Your son is going to live";
and he believed, he and his whole household. (54) This, again, is the
second sign Jesus did after coming out of Judea into Galilee.

John ties this miracle quite explicitly to the first sign at Cana—
by noting their common location, by reminding us of the first
one in v. 46, and by numbering them consecutively. We should
look then for some fundamental analogy between the two stories,
and it is not far to seek. In each story, someone asks Jesus to meet
a human need; he rebuffs the petitioner, who then returns to the
issue without any apology; and Jesus performs the miracle. The
principal difference is that, at this point in the Gospel, the issues
of belief have been explored more fully and the problem can be
laid out more clearly in the story itself. What Jesus rebuffs is the
assumption that miracles produce belief; they do produce public
interest, but no reliable sort of attachment to Jesus. Still, the
father's persistence represents a kind of belief in itself; like Mary
in the earlier story, he acknowledges that there is nowhere else
to turn. Thus, when Jesus tells him that his son is going to live,
he believes, at some level, without first having to witness the
miracle. Perhaps there is a hint here of the teaching in Mark's
Gospel that faith is vital to healings. In any case, the miracle
takes place. It is confirmed, as in the case of the wine, by the
evidence of nobodies (servants there, slaves here) whose witness
would hardly count in court. It can scarcely prove anything at all.

This story, in itself, has nothing to do with baptism. It is placed
here, however, to introduce a theological discourse and to provide

a foil for the following story, which has some rather unpleasant news about the value of external signs:

(5:1) After these things, there was a feast of the Jews, and Jesus went up to Jerusalem. (2) Now, there is a pool in Jerusalem by the sheep-gate called, in Hebrew, Bethzatha. It has five porticoes. (3) In these porticoes used to lie a multitude of sick people—blind, lame, par-alyzed; (5) and there was one person there who had been sick thirty-eight years. (6) When Jesus saw this man lying there and recognized that he had already been there a long time, he says to him, "Do you want to get well?" (7) The sick man answered him, "Sir, I don't have anybody to throw me into the pool whenever the water is stirred up; and while I'm going, someone else gets down ahead of me." (8) Jesus says to him, "Get up, pick up your cot, and walk." (9a) And at once the man got well, and he picked up his cot and went walking about.

Up to this point, we are dealing with a fairly standard miracle story—close enough, at least, that certain peculiarities stand out. The first is that the miracle takes place at Jesus' initiative, not that of the person in need. (It will later appear that the paralytic does not even know who Jesus is.) This is not only unusual in comparison with miracle stories in the Synoptic Gospels; it is quite unlike the two Cana miracles, too. The second is that there is no one, apparently, to know of it except Jesus and the paralytic himself. (There is no public amazement, as in the Synoptics, nor private knowledge among the servants or the slaves as in the Cana miracles.) There has also been no reference of any kind to be-lieving, a subject so important in the preceding miracle. All this would seem to make the miracle a fine example of a revelatory sign—an unknown Jesus passes by, heals the paralytic, and is then recognized for who he truly is. As we shall see, however, it does not work this way.

This narrative is primarily preparation for the theological dis-course that will follow it. The rather full description of the pool, however, shows that John has not dropped the subject of baptism. The pool, after all, is a kind of baptism,[10] thought to cure people (though perhaps only at odd moments when the waters were "stirred up").[11] In the crush of those moments, however, it is possible to get left out; others get into the water first and either fill the pool or block the way for the paralytic until the bubbling stops. Since John's Jesus was so emphatic earlier about the need to be born of water and wind, one might expect a similar reverence here for the externals of faith; Jesus might, for example, help the man into the pool himself. Instead, he extends a kind of special privilege, bypassing the baptism. For John, the outward and visible sign, however important he deems it, has no monopoly on transactions between God and humanity. God is free to act directly, and it is the inner reality that is vital. (We shall see a similar motif in chapter 6 in relation to the theme of Eucharist.)

Even God's direct action in healing or in granting rebirth proves inconclusive, however, in terms of its effect on human beings. Just as conversion is no reliable indicator of future loyalty, so rebirth in baptism (here imaged in the paralytic's restoration to health) guarantees nothing. The newly healed man turns informer:

> (5:9b) Now it was Sabbath that day. (10) So the Jews said to the man who had been healed, "It's Sabbath, and you're not permitted to pick up your cot." (11) And he answered them, "The one who made me well, that one said to me, 'Pick up your cot and walk.'" (12) They asked him, "Who is the person that told you, 'Pick it up and walk'?" (13) But the man who had been treated did not know who it was, for Jesus had slipped from sight (there was a crowd in the place). (14) Later, Jesus finds him in the temple and told him, "See, you've gotten well. Stop sinning now, or something worse might happen to you." (15) The fellow went and reported to the Jews that Jesus was the one who had made him well. (16) And for this reason the Jews were persecuting Jesus because he would do these things on the Sabbath.

The paralytic finds himself in an awkward predicament over breaking the Sabbath law. We must imagine his gratitude for being healed in conflict with his irritation at the fact that Jesus has made him break the law in the process. Jesus subsequently warns him to stop sinning, which must seem to add insult to injury. Yet, he then goes out to commit the one real sin there is—unfaith. He promptly deserts the man who has cured him of a thirty-eight-year-long illness and gratuitously and unnecessarily denounces him. Thus, the baptized may prove to be loyal witnesses, like the Samaritan woman, or betrayers, like the paralytic. Jesus' power to help and transform through the external sign does not predetermine the human results.

The increased tension with the Jewish authorities, however, does give John an opportunity to introduce a theological discourse, this time clearly in the mouth of Jesus himself. This is the first in a series that one might appropriately call the "obnoxious discourses," for the claims Jesus makes in them are so extravagant that one is forced to adopt some kind of serious stance for or against him. In this way, he renders himself more and more obnoxious to the authorities. Yet, for the reader, the content of these discourses is nothing more than a continued working out of the implications of the prologue.

> (5:17) But Jesus answered them, "My father is working right up to now—and I am working." (18) For this reason, then, the Jews tried still more to kill him, because he not only broke the Sabbath but even called God his own father, making himself equal to God.

Jesus' claim to divinity is still rather vague at this point, but his opponents catch it. His justification for breaking the Sabbath is to claim that the Sabbath itself is based on false premises, that is, that Gen. 2:2–3 is mistaken in claiming that the work of creation is over. Jesus had already hinted as much to his disciples (4:34) when he spoke of "finishing God's work." When Jesus goes on to associate his own work closely with the father's, he is reiterating John's theological premise that the logos was and is the only link between God and the creation.

It may be useful here to review some previous instances of this theme. In the first miracle at Cana and in the clearing out of the temple, Jesus substituted himself for the religious forms of Judaism, as if to say that there is no access to God that does not go through him. In the theological discourses that follow the Nicodemus episode (3:16–21, 31–36), believing in the son becomes the touchstone of good and evil—and therefore of ultimate judgment—among human beings. In this way, the son also becomes the key to everlasting life. It is this last element that will now be expanded:

> (5:19) Jesus, then, replied and said to them, "Amen, amen, I say to you, the son cannot do anything on his own unless it's something he sees the father doing. For whatever things that one does, these the son, too, does in the same way. (20) For the father loves the son and shows him all the things that he himself does; and he will show him greater works than these, so that you will be taken by surprise. (21) For just as the father raises the dead and brings them to life, so too the son brings those whom he wishes to life. (22) For the father doesn't even judge anyone, but has handed all judgment over to the son, (23) so that all may honor the son just as they honor the father. The one who doesn't honor the son doesn't honor the father that sent him.
>
> (24) "Amen, amen, I say to you, the one who hears what I say and believes the one who sent me has everlasting life—and doesn't come under judgment, but has crossed over from death into life.
>
> (25) "Amen, amen, I say to you, an hour is coming—and it's here

now—when the dead will hear the voice of God's son and those who
have heard it will live. (26) For just as the father has life in himself,
so too he has granted the son to have life in himself. (27) And he
has granted him power to pass judgment because he is son of humanity. (28) Don't be surprised at this, because an hour is coming
when all those who are in the tombs will hear his voice. (29) And
they will come out, those who've done good things to a resurrection
of life and those who've done bad to a resurrection of judgment. (30)
I cannot do anything on my own; I judge just the way I hear. And
my judgment is correct, because I don't aim at my own will, but at
the will of the one who has sent me.

This discourse requires little comment, for it is simply the eschatological equivalent of the prologue's doctrine of creation. Or,
to put it less technically, Jesus is here painted as possessing the
same absolute, God-derived authority over the end of human existence as over its beginning. He "has life in himself" (as we had
already read in 1:4); under God, he has the ability to summon the
dead to life. Only one new element is added: as son of humanity,
he will also be their judge. As son of God he was sent to save,
not to judge (3:16–17); and yet the results are much the same. If
he is indeed that only link, the logos, the son, between God and
us, then our attitude toward him and his work (an attitude manifest in our own works) will inevitably judge us.

Such grandiose claims inevitably lead to the question of evidence. Why should the authorities take Jesus seriously? The answer is difficult and ambiguous:

(5:31) "If I testify about myself, my testimony isn't true. (32) There's
another person who testifies about me, and I know that the testimony that person testifies about me *is* true. (33) You people sent to
John, and he testified to the truth. (34) Now, *I* don't accept testimony from a human being, but I'm telling you these things so that
you may be saved. (35) That man was the burning and shining lamp,
but you were unwilling to celebrate for an hour in his light.

(36) "But *I* have the testimony better than John's, for the works
that the father has given me to finish—the very works that I do—
testify of me that the father has sent me. (37) And the father who
sent me—that one has testified about me. You've never heard his
voice nor seen his form, (38) and you don't have his word staying in
you, because you don't believe the person whom that one has sent.
(39) Inquire of the writings, because *you* suppose that you have everlasting life in *them*—and those are what testify about me! (40) And
you're not willing to come to me to get life.

The whole question of evidence is circular. Once accept Jesus as
God's son, and everything "testifies to him": John the Baptist,

his own works (not, presumably, just the miracles, but everything he does), God, the scriptures. On the other hand, reject Jesus and none of these witnesses any longer has its true meaning. Jesus claims a central place in reality; he is the keystone of all meaning. Yet, his claims cannot breach his opponents' defenses. They are basically unwilling to approach him and this unwillingness can be traced to a more fundamental flaw:

> (5:41) "I don't accept glory from human beings. (42) But I know you— you don't have God's love in yourselves. (43) I've come in my father's name and you don't accept me; if someone else comes in his own name, you'll accept that one! (44) How *can* you believe, when you accept glory from each other and don't look for the glory that comes from God alone? (45) Don't suppose that *I'll* accuse you before the father; your accuser is Moses, in whom you have put your hope. (46) For if you had believed Moses, you would have believed me, for it's of me that that man wrote. (47) But if you don't believe his writings, how will you believe my words?"

In this peroration, Jesus seems to set his opponents permanently beyond the pale. It is their earlier and internal failure to take God, or even Moses, seriously which leads to the subsequent and external failure to recognize Jesus for who he is. All judgment is merely a response to the reality of the person being judged.

The section on baptism is a long one, combining a discussion of baptism itself with warnings that it does not produce indefectibility and also with an expansion of John's basic theological premise about the central role of the logos. John's Jesus has proclaimed the absolute necessity of being reborn through water and spirit—and also implied that the essential thing is not the outer rite, but the inner reality of being filled with Jesus' truth.[12] The believer comes to recognize the son as both origin and end of human life, and then becomes a means by which others, too, may come to know him. But unbelievers suffer from some fundamental inward block, which shuts out every kind of testimony and seems to render them impervious to the truth. Is this simply abuse flung at the opponents of the Johannine community? Hardly. It is a statement about human realities, for John recognizes that the baptized are as prone to betrayal as the unbaptized are to unbelief.

4

EUCHARIST

(John 6:1—7:52)

Early Christian converts, once initiated into the church through Baptism, became participants in the community's sacred meal: the Lord's Supper or Eucharist. Indeed, from an early time the Eucharist formed an integral part of the initiation rites, with the new Christians receiving it immediately after their Baptism.[1] John, as we have noted earlier, has no narrative of the institution of the Eucharist in his account of the Last Supper (chaps. 13—17). It is unlikely that he did not know the tradition, for he seems to echo parts of it in his chapter 6. He does not narrate it at the usual place, however, because of his desire to place the major treatment of Eucharist in the sequence of the believer's personal experience of it.

Since there was another meal-tradition about Jesus, which could carry eucharistic overtones even in the Synoptic versions of it, John was able to make use of it to introduce the subject:[2]

(6:1) After these events, Jesus went off across the Sea of Galilee (that is, of Tiberias). (2) And there was a big crowd following, as they saw the signs he was performing on the sick. (3) But Jesus went up on the mountain and took a seat there with his disciples. (4) (Now it was close to the passover, the Jews' festival.) (5) When Jesus, then, had raised his eyes and observed that a big crowd was coming toward him, he says to Philip, "Where are we to buy bread for these people to eat?" (6) (Now, he was testing him when he said this, for he himself knew what he was going to do.) (7) Philip answered him, "Two hundred denarii worth of bread wouldn't be enough for them, for everybody to get just a little." (8) One of his disciples, Andrew, Simon Peter's brother, tells him, (9) "There's a child here that has five barley loaves and two fish, but what do these amount to with so many people?" (10) Jesus said, "Have the people lie down to eat." (There was a lot of grass in the place.) So the men lay down—about five thousand in number. (11) So Jesus took the loaves and, after giving thanks, shared them with the people lying there. The same, too, with the fish—as much as they wanted. (12) And when they were full, he says to his disciples, "Gather up the leftover fragments, so that nothing gets lost." (13) So they gathered them up and filled twelve baskets with fragments from the five barley loaves—what was left over by the people who had eaten. (14) The people, then, when they saw what sign he had done were saying, "This really is the prophet who was to come into the cosmos." (15) So when Jesus recognized that they were about to come and seize him to make him king, he withdrew again to the mountain, entirely by himself.

There are interesting differences here from the Synoptic versions of the story. Jesus does not teach this crowd, nor do they come to hear his teaching. They are there for one reason only— because they are interested in signs; and Jesus will exercise the same caution toward them as toward others similarly attracted to him (2:23–25). He does, however, perform a great miracle, and his audience takes it as a particularly revealing one. When they deduce that he is "prophet," they may be thinking of the similar miracle that Elisha performed with barley loaves (2 Kings 4:42– 44). Or, since they specify "the prophet who was to come," they may be thinking of Moses' role in supplying the manna in the wasteland (Exodus 16)—a topic they will return to later in this chapter (6:31). There may also be, in their reaction, a hint of the great eschatological banquet which appears in Isaiah 25 as symbol of God's final triumph over evil. Whatever the background, the crowd interprets the miracle in a way that Jesus will not accept, and he withdraws (or, according to some ancient texts, "escapes") to the mountain.

The disciples here do not come off much better than the crowd. Jesus tests Philip by questioning him about local markets; Philip responds by complaining about the staggering expense of feeding such a crowd. (The sum he names was apparently about two-thirds of a day laborer's maximum yearly income.) Andrew has done a little practical survey of the resources and reports what he has found, but doubts that his report is relevant. What this shows about both disciples is that, even though they have been with him from the start, they have not yet really understood who Jesus is. The one who created the universe is not to be stymied by a problem of such minor magnitude. There is a sharp contrast with the behavior of Jesus' mother and of the royal official in the

Cana miracles: they refused to look anywhere but to Jesus for relief; the disciples, admittedly with Jesus' own ironic prompting, look everywhere except to him.

The following story reinforces this picture of the disciples' failure:

> (6:16) Now, when it got late, the disciples went down by the sea, (17) got on board a boat, and started across the sea to Capernaum. (And it had already gotten dark and Jesus had not yet come to them.) (18) And the sea got up, with a high wind blowing. (19) So when they had rowed about three miles or a little more, they observe Jesus walking on the sea and getting near the boat; and they were frightened. (20) But he says to them, "It's I. Don't be afraid." (21) So they wanted to take him into the boat, and at once the boat arrived at the land where they were headed.

This story is told quite differently in each of the three Gospels that recount it (Matthew, Mark, John). John's version emphasizes several points. The first is that Jesus has left the disciples to their own devices (not deliberately sent them on ahead as in Matthew and Mark); their response to being abandoned is not to wait for Jesus, but to head back to a familiar place. This may not, in itself, be reprehensible; but one remembers that they failed to take him with appropriate seriousness in the preceding narrative. The second point is that they did this in the dark—a symbolic motif which again suggests that they are still basically out of touch with Jesus' true being and work. Third, when they do see Jesus, they are afraid. Apparently, they have no notion as yet, despite the two miracles at Cana and the great feeding, that he is the creator and that he has full command of the elements. Finally, their encounter with him produces a curious and perplexing distortion of space and time. They were only about halfway to their destination when they encountered him; yet, they no sooner try to take him on board than they find they have reached the land.

The physical disorientation implied in this incident, however, is no greater than the religious one which the following discourse will produce:

> (6:22) The next day, the crowd, still on the other side of the sea, saw that there had only been one boat there and that Jesus had not gotten on board the boat with his disciples but his disciples had left by themselves. (23) Other boats, out of Tiberias, came near the place where they had eaten the bread after the Lord gave thanks. (24) When the crowd saw, then, that Jesus was not there, nor his disciples, they, too, got on board the boats and came to Capernaum looking for Jesus.

(25) And when they found him on this side of the sea, they said to him, "Rabbi, when did you get here?" (26) Jesus responded and said to them, "Amen, amen, I say to you, you're not looking for me because you saw signs but because you ate some bread and were satisfied. (27) Don't keep working on the food that perishes, but on the food that lasts into everlasting life—the son of humanity will give it to you. For the father, God, has certified this one." (28) So they said to him, "What are we to do in order to be working God's works?" (29) Jesus answered and told them, "This is God's work—to believe in the person whom that one has sent." (30) So they said to him, "What sign are *you* doing, then, for us to see it and believe you? What are you working on? (31) Our ancestors ate the manna in the wasteland, just as it's written: 'He gave them bread from heaven to eat.'" (32) So Jesus said to them, "Amen, amen, I say to you, it wasn't Moses that gave you the bread from heaven; but my father gives you the real bread from heaven. (33) For God's bread is the one that comes down from heaven and gives life to the cosmos."

The crowds are as perplexed at Jesus' curious mobility as the disciples must be. Perhaps it may be another sign. But when they obliquely ask for an explanation ("When did you get here?" not "How?"), Jesus answers with an "inappropriate response." He ignores their question and charges them with a purely prudential interest in him. They followed him across the lake originally because they were interested in signs. That was little enough; but now even that motive is gone and they care only for free food. Jesus responds, "You still have to work for your food, but make sure it is the right food and the right employer." (The word translated "will give" in v. 27 does not necessarily imply a free gift in Greek; it is also used of making contractual payments.)

Jesus is, of course, pointing to himself as source of real life. The crowd does not yet sense this, but picks up his reference to God as the ultimate source of food and asks how one can be sure of being on God's right side. The only thing that matters, says Jesus, is to believe in the one whom God has sent. Now, the crowd sees that Jesus is making himself the key figure; but they are skeptical. Or perhaps they simply see the possibility of getting something for themselves in exchange. You must prove yourself, they say; and it would be perfectly appropriate for you to do that by providing more food. After all, God gave the people free manna when they were wandering in the wasteland of Sinai! Jesus, in a sense, agrees with them: the manna was not tied to Moses or to a past time in history; my father is giving it now.

The crowd, like the Samaritan woman in the midst of her conversation with Jesus, thinks the situation is now clear; and they respond accordingly:

(6:34) So they said to him, "Sir, give us this bread all the time." (35) Jesus said to them, "*I* am the bread of life. The one who comes to me will never get hungry, and the one who believes in me will never get thirsty at any time. (36) But I've told you that you *have* seen it and still you don't believe.

(37) "Everything that the father gives me will come to me, and I will never throw the one who comes to me out, (38) because I've come down from heaven not to do what I want, but what the one who has sent me wants. (39) And this is what the one who has sent me wants: that I should not lose anything out of all he's given me, but should raise it up at the last day. (40) For this is what my father wants: that everybody who perceives the son and believes in him should have everlasting life, and I should raise him up at the last day."

As throughout the book, John redirects our attention from externalities, even such essentials as food, to the one central fact of the logos or son, through whom all things exist and without whom there is nothing. If life is in the logos, then it is no difficulty for Jesus to say, "*I* am the bread of life." This is the first of a series of great metaphors which sum up Jesus' absolute centrality for human life; they take the form of emphatic I-statements (more emphatic in Greek than one can readily convey in English). In uttering this "*I* am . . . ," Jesus sweeps away the crowd's concern for literal food; that is a secondary level of reality. The one who is in full relationship with the son can never get hungry or thirsty again—a strong echo of what Jesus has said to the Samaritan woman in 4:14.

The reason behind this claim appears in an expansion of an earlier theological statement. In 3:16, John had declared that God sent the son to save all who believe. Jesus now reaffirms that. The whole point of his coming is to lose nothing of what has been entrusted to him. He says this first in the neuter, speaking of things, then again in the masculine, which is here the Greek common gender denoting persons in general. This leaves open the question whether there are some things and some people who have not been entrusted to him and may therefore be lost. We have already seen some wrestling with this problem in the obnoxious discourse of 5:19–47. Probably, John would say yes, that there are some who are beyond hope. At least, the next passage suggests that God is free to work in such a way.

The audience, however, has barely heard the rationale for Jesus' claims; the claims themselves are more than they can accept.

(6:41) The Jews, then, were muttering about him because he said, "I am the bread that has come down from heaven"; (42) and they were saying, "Isn't this Jesus son of Joseph? We know his father and mother! How can he say now, 'I've come down from heaven'?" (43) Jesus responded and said to them, "Don't keep muttering to one another. (44) No one can come to me unless the father who sent me draws him; and *I* will raise him up on the last day. (45) It's written in the prophets, 'And they will all be God-instructed.' Everybody who has heard and learned from the father comes to me. (46) Not that anyone has seen the father except for the one who is from God— this one has seen the father.

Jesus' response to doubts here is continuous with what he had to say in chapter 5. All response to his teaching depends on God's direct intervention with the hearer. This does not mean, however, that this direct intervention takes the place of Jesus as mediator. Others may hear and learn from God, but only the son has *seen* the father and possesses full knowledge.

With this, we return to the theme of bread. Jesus has already created problems by identifying the bread with himself. The opponents, not knowing his true origins as we, the readers, do, cannot accept the notion that he has some absolute relationship with God or with human life. In the spirit and tradition of the obnoxious discourses, Jesus goes on to make the problems more, not less, acute:

(6:47) "Amen, amen, I say to you, the one who believes has everlasting life. (48) *I* am the bread of life. (49) Your ancestors ate the manna in the wasteland and died; (50) this is the bread that comes down from heaven so that one may eat from it and not die. (51) *I* am the living bread that has come down from heaven; if anyone eats from this bread he will live for ever. And the bread that I will give is my flesh—for the life of the cosmos."

As life depends on food, so everlasting life depends on *the* bread of life. This is not anything of the created order, such as the manna was, but something that obliterates the boundary of this creation, which is death.[3] Jesus thus repeats his self-identification as "bread of life" a second time; but the third time, by a minor shift, the phrase has become "living bread," which leads directly to the repugnant, indeed cannibalistic challenge of his closing statement. The original reader, a Christian initiate, will of course have understood this as a eucharistic reference; but Jesus' immediate audience cannot do so.

The opponents object, understandably enough; and in response, Jesus makes it all worse:

> (6:52) So the Jews started fighting with each other, saying "How can this man give us his flesh to eat?" (53) So Jesus said to them, "Amen, amen, I say to you, unless you eat the flesh of the son of humanity and drink his blood, you don't have life in yourselves. (54) The one who chews my flesh and drinks my blood has everlasting life; and *I* will raise him up at the last day, (55) for my flesh is real food and my blood is real drink. (56) The one who chews my flesh and drinks my blood stays in me and I in him. (57) Just as the living father has sent me and I live because of the father, the one who chews me— yes, that one, too—will live because of me. (58) This is the bread that has come down from heaven—not the way the ancestors ate and died; the one who chews this bread will live for ever." (59) He said these things while teaching in synagogue at Capernaum.

In this part of the argument, Jesus substitutes the coarser word "chew" for the more general "eat," thus making the image still more concrete and therefore more repugnant. He also introduces new language about drinking his blood—a eucharistic reference for the Christian reader, but an additional obscenity for the opponents. The Torah, after all, forbids all consumption of blood (Gen. 9:4); how much worse, then, is the idea of drinking human blood? Yet, Jesus insists (in a way familiar to us by now) that this is the only point of access to God. In language that recalls the prologue, Jesus traces a line of derivation from the father to himself to the believer. This is how life comes from the only one who is truly, absolutely, and originally alive ("the living father") to the human creature. In one sense, the whole cosmos already participates in this life; yet, there is another sense in which the creation is now dead and has yet to be raised to complete life in the last day.

It is hardly surprising, of course, that Jesus' opponents do not accept these teachings; they seem to overthrow too much of the Torah. (The contrast is underlined by John's note that Jesus uttered all this while teaching in synagogue.) A more surprising result of the discussion is that many of his own disciples find these teachings insupportable.

> (6:60) Many of his disciples, then, when they heard it, said, "This is a hard saying. Who can listen to it?" (61) But Jesus recognized within himself that his disciples were muttering about this and said

to them, "Does this make you stumble? (62) What, then, if you should observe the son of humanity going back up where he was before? (63) The spirit is what gives life; the flesh does no good at all. The words that I've spoken to you—they are spirit and they are life. (64) But there are some of you who don't believe." (For Jesus knew from the start who they were who did not believe and who it was that would betray him. (65) And he used to say, "This is why I've told you that no one can come to me unless it's been granted him from the father.") (66) As a result of this, many of his disciples left and went back and would not travel with him any longer. (67) So Jesus said to the Twelve, "Do you wish to go, too?" (68) Simon Peter answered him, "Sir, to whom would we go? You have words of everlasting life, (69) and we have believed and recognized that you are God's holy one." (70) Jesus replied to them, "Didn't I choose you as the Twelve? And one of you is a devil." (71) Now, he was talking about Judas son of Simon Iscariot, for this was the man who would betray him—one of the Twelve.

We saw a hint, in the episode at the Pool of Bethzatha, that Baptism (or its equivalent), while necessary for the Christian life, does not guarantee the loyalty of those who receive it. Subsequently, we saw that even Philip and Andrew, two of Jesus' earliest converts, failed in some respects in the episode of the great feeding. In the present discussion, this problem is made fully explicit: even the fully initiated, those who have participated in the Eucharist, are not perfectly reliable. Many of Jesus' disciples leave because of his outrageous language; and among those who remain, even within the inner circle of the Twelve, is the betrayer. John mentions that detail three times in eight verses to be sure we do not miss the point.[4]

And what is the point, exactly? That external realities do not determine internal ones; only the gift of God can do that. "The spirit is what gives life; the flesh does no good at all." Coming on the heels of Jesus' earlier claims for those who would "chew his flesh," this statement seems out of place. It is consistent, however, with John's overall view of the progress of the Christian mystic. "Does this make you stumble? What, then, if you should observe the son of humanity going back up where he was before?" As with Nicodemus (3:12), these are but the earthly realities; the heavenly ones are correspondingly more difficult. The sacraments are indeed an essential step for the believer in becoming related to Jesus. Yet, they are not ends in themselves, nor are they a sufficient cause of salvation.

What is the sufficient cause? Who can say? "The wind blows

where it likes, and you hear its sound, but you don't know where it's coming from and where it's going. That's how it is with everyone that is born of the wind" (3:8). "No one can come to me unless it's been granted him from the father" (6:65). The one possible clue is in the words of Jesus, for if anything can cross the boundary between outer and inner it is they (6:63). This is not to say that words are more reliable than other signs; otherwise, one could hardly explain the continuing intransigence of the opponents—or Jesus' habitual refusal to make his teaching verbally clearer or more attractive. No, it is simply that words can sometimes get around the familiar and take us by surprise, as unexpectedly as the spirit itself.

At this point, we move from discussion of the Eucharist back to the more strictly theological development of the Gospel—a further exploration of what it means to say that Jesus is the only link between God and humanity. John makes the transition with a further, if oblique, discussion of outer and inner, of signs and words:

> (7:1) And after these things, Jesus was traveling in Galilee, for he was unwilling to travel in Judea because the Jews were looking for him to kill him. (2) And the Jews' feast of Tabernacles was soon. (3) So his brothers said to him, "Move on from here and go to Judea, so that your disciples, too, will observe the works that you're doing. (4) For no one does anything secretly and expects to be spoken of publicly. If you're doing these things, reveal yourself to the cosmos." (5) For not even his brothers believed in him. (6) So Jesus says to them, "My time isn't here yet, but your time is always at hand. (7) The cosmos cannot hate you, but it hates me because I testify of it that its actions are evil. (8) *You* go up to the feast. *I'm* not going up to this feast because my time isn't fulfilled yet." (9) And having said these things, he stayed in Galilee. (10) But when his brothers had gone up to the feast, then he himself went up, too—not openly, but secretly. (11) The Jews, then, were looking for him at the feast and saying, "Where is that man?" (12) And there was a lot of muttering about him in the crowd. Some were saying, "He's a good man"; others were saying, "No! He's misleading the crowd." (13) Yet, no one would talk openly about him for fear of the Jews.

Hitherto, Jesus had worked miracles in Jerusalem, and his brothers assume that he has disciples there. That, they believe, is as it should be. Great figures do not stick around country crossroads; they make their presence felt in the capital. He has done it before and now he should be doing it again. The brothers are supporters of Jesus in a sense; but they do not "believe" (that is, understand who Jesus really is) and therefore see only the externals of his ministry. Jesus replies that their interests reflect an orientation exactly opposite his own and that he will not go.

Yet, he does go—though without altering the behavior that his brothers have objected to. He goes up "secretly" (v. 10, cf. v. 4), not "openly" (same Greek root as in "reveal yourself," v. 4). And the situation remains just as his brothers complained: they want him to be a subject of public discussion (*en parrhēsia*, v. 4), but at most there is only muttering in the crowd, with no one speaking "openly" (same Greek phrase, v. 13). Jesus goes up, it seems, not only secretly, but entirely by himself; we do not find him in the company of his disciples again until chapter 11.[5]

He goes up not to work signs, but to talk. Is this to be a demonstration of word-as-spirit? (Cf. 6:63.) If so, it is a curious one, for again we are in the realm of the obnoxious discourse, designed less to convert than to alienate:

(7:14) And when the feast was already half over, Jesus went up to the temple and was teaching. (15) So the Jews were surprised, saying, "How does this person know literature without having been someone's disciple?" (16) Jesus then answered them and said, "My teaching is not mine but belongs to the one who sent me. (17) If anyone is willing to do what he wants, he will know with regard to the teaching whether it is from God or whether I'm talking on my own. (18) The person who talks on his own is looking for glory for himself; but the one who aims at glory for the one that sent him—this one is true and there is no injustice in him.

Jesus goes unrecognized at first, making an impression only by his teaching. This creates a problem for the authorities when they cannot place him in a chain of discipleship like that claimed for the rabbis.[6] If he is a self-taught person, he must be suspect. Jesus replies that the real issue is one of honor: does he want it for himself or for someone else? He is like the rabbis in crediting his teacher, but he hints (in a way clear enough for the reader) that this teacher is God. The discussion thus picks up from the discourse that followed the healing at Bethzatha, almost as if Jesus had never been away; for there, too, he had claimed God as his only teacher (5:19–29).

Jesus had also claimed then that Moses would be his opponents' accuser (5:45–47), and he now returns to the theme that the religion of his opponents is not really that of Moses at all.

(7:19) "Didn't Moses give you the law? And not one of you keeps the law. Why are you looking for me to kill me?" (20) The crowd replied, "You have a demon! Who's looking for you to kill you?" (21) Jesus answered and said to them, "I've done one work, and you're all taken by surprise. (22) This is why Moses gave you the rite of circumcision—not that it's from Moses, but from the ancestors—and you circumcise a person on Sabbath. (23) If a person gets circumcised on Sabbath so as not to break the law of Moses, can you get angry with me because I made a whole person healthy on Sabbath? (24) Don't judge by appearances, but give a correct judgment."

Jesus hints at his identity by referring to the incident at Bethzatha, which was a violation of the Sabbath law (one of the fundamental Ten Commandments). Yet, he argues that it is wrong to treat what he did as a crime, and he produces a legal argument to show that there are appropriate exceptions to the Sabbath law. If it is permissible to circumcise on Sabbath, it is all the more permissible to make a whole person healthy. The attack on him is therefore actually a violation, not a defense, of Torah. What appears to be a crime is lawful; what appears to be zeal for Torah is a crime. "Don't judge by appearances."

Jesus makes little progress with his audience, however, as the following shows:

(7:25) Some of the Jerusalemites were saying, "Isn't this the man they were looking for to kill? (26) And see! he's talking openly and they're not saying a thing to him. Do you suppose that the members of the Council really know that this man is the anointed? (27) But we know where this man is from! And when the anointed comes, nobody knows where he's from." (28) Jesus, therefore, shouted aloud in the temple, teaching and saying, "So you know me and you know where I'm from! And I haven't come from myself, but the one who sent me is true. You don't know him. (29) I know him because I am from him and that's the one who sent me." (30) They were looking for him, then, to arrest him, but nobody laid a hand on him because his hour had not yet come. (31) But many people from the crowd believed in him and were saying, "When the anointed does come, will he do more signs than this man has done?"

The crowd's dependence on external signs takes an ironic turn, for the external indicators themselves are contradictory. The authorities' failure to arrest him might be an indication of secret recognition. Jesus' miracles argue in favor of his claims, and some are still swayed by them. Yet, his origins argue against him, as Nathanael (1:46) and the Galilean crowds (6:41–42) have already said. Jesus merely mocks their confusion: So you know so much, do you?

This sort of discussion will lead nowhere. And the audience should know that the questions will get more, not less, difficult to resolve.

(7:32) The Pharisees heard the crowd muttering these things about him; and the chief priests and the Pharisees sent servants to arrest him. (33) So Jesus said, "I'm with you a little while yet, and I'm going to the one who sent me. (34) You'll look for me and you won't find me; and you cannot come where I am." (35) So the Jews said among themselves, "Where is this man going to go that we won't find him? Is he going to go into the diaspora of the Greeks and teach the Greeks? (36) What is this claim that he's made—'You'll look for me and you won't find me, and you cannot come where I am'?"

Jesus, the sole point of access between humanity and God, is proving, at this juncture, inaccessible to his opponents. They cannot come where he *is*.[7] He is permanently beyond their grasp and he will, if anything, move further away. They interpret this claim in spatial terms: will he make a tour of the Greek-speaking Jewish communities? It is conceivable, for he has already crossed a more significant social barrier to reach the Samaritans. Yet, that is beside the point now. The cosmos cannot reach him at all, even though it has no being except through him, because it persists in its alienation from God. No one can come to him except as it is granted by the father.

John now brings Jesus' proclamation to a close with a final passage which looks both forward and back. It is phrased in terms not unlike those Jesus used with the Samaritan woman:

(7:37) On the last day of the feast, the great day, Jesus stood and shouted, saying, "If anyone is thirsty, come to me and drink. (38) The one who believes in me—just as it says in writing, 'Rivers of living water will flow out of his belly.'" (39) But he said this with reference to the spirit which those who had believed in him would receive. For there was no spirit as yet, because Jesus had not yet been glorified.

The imagery is grotesque, as in the cannibalistic language of chapter 6; but this time John has nothing to gain by exploiting its oddity. He simply affirms that the believer, like Jesus himself, will have an unbounded life-giving power within, quite inaccessible to external observation. The claim that this promise is "in writing," that is, scriptural, is difficult, as the source of the quotation is not known.[8] Still, the authority of the pronouncement is that of God's logos, not of scripture. The important thing is that believing confers this life-giving power, not external rites of Baptism or Eucharist.

The real meaning of the saying has to do, therefore, with the spirit, the hidden, inner reality of the believer's life. This spirit can come only when the tangible, physical, historical Jesus departs, as we shall see later (16:7), for it constitutes an inward communion with father and son that is not accessible to outward verification. This message, however, is lost on Jesus' audience. He is now so far beyond what the cosmos can hear that, even though he shouts it at the feast, it makes little impression. Most of the crowd, together with the officials, turn back to the insoluble problem of external evidences:

(7:40) So some from the crowd, once they heard these words, were saying, "This man really is the prophet." (41) Others said, "This man is the anointed," while still others said, "What?! Does the anointed come from Galilee? (42) Hasn't the writing said that the anointed comes of the seed of David—and from Bethlehem, the town where David was?" (43) Thus a split developed in the crowd on account of him. (44) And some of them wanted to arrest him, but nobody laid hands on him.

Some people in the crowd are again exercised by the problem of origins. A new element here is the suggestion that the Messiah should, after all, have come from Bethlehem. Though John never refers to Jesus' birthplace, a reader of the Gospel who knew no other traditions on the matter would probably assume that it was Nazareth. Since John's first readers, however, were already Christians, it is at least possible that they thought of Jesus as having been born at Bethlehem, for both Matthew and Luke independently record such traditions. If this was known to the Johannine church, too, the Christian readers will be laughing up their sleeves at the progressive stupidity of Jesus' opponents.[9] Whichever may be the case, the point remains the same: Jesus can be truly known only by his inner truth, that is, by his connection to the father and to the creation. All else is inconsequential detail.

Still, it is appropriate, in John's view, if those who do not know *the* truth also make petty mistakes as well. Thus, he allows the authorities to make an ironic mistake about their own membership:

(7:45) So the servants came to the chief priests and Pharisees; and those people said to them, "Why haven't you brought him?" (46) The servants answered, "Nobody has ever talked this way!" (47) The

Pharisees then responded to them, "Have you been misled, too? (48) Has a single member of the Council believed in him or any of the Pharisees? (49) But this crowd that is ignorant of the law—they're accursed." (50) Nicodemus, the man who came to him previously, who was one of them, says to them, (51) "Does our law judge the person without first hearing from him and learning what he does?" (52) They replied and said to him, "Are you from Galilee, too? Investigate and see that no prophet arises from Galilee."

The servants found it impossible to arrest Jesus because the crowd had split over him; and the authorities, powerless against him for the moment, can only swear at the interfering mob. They boast that their own number, at least, is immune; but the reader already knows from chapter 3 that this is wrong. To underline their mistake, John brings Nicodemus back onstage for a mild and, as it turns out, fruitless protest against the proceedings. The only thing that is important to the opponents now is Jesus' Galilean origin, which is their "proof" that he is of negligible religious importance.

The section on the Eucharist thus ends on a note of confusion. As the means of approach to Jesus (conversion, Baptism, Eucharist) mount up, they also become, strangely, less useful. They do not guarantee the faithfulness of those who have passed through them (Judas the supreme example) and they mean nothing to the opponents. The latter are becoming more resolute in their rejection of Jesus, though their reasons show a decaying grasp of the religious realities involved. Jesus himself makes no effort to help. He expresses himself in shocking terminology; he accuses his opponents of crimes against the Law; he builds no bridges. John is saying that one must accept Jesus on his terms or not at all; lesser levels of reality cannot be used to prove or disprove the truth about the logos.

The material which now follows, in chapter 8, continues in the style of "obnoxious discourse." Indeed, there is little narrative division between the two chapters. Since the servants failed to arrest Jesus in chapter 7, he simply goes on teaching in public. (The widespread placement of the story of the woman taken in adultery at just this point may suggest, however, that at least one ancient scribe detected a break in continuity here.) Up to this point John has begun each section with a narrative pertaining to its special subject matter: for conversion, the making of the first disciples; for Baptism, Nicodemus' visit; for Eucharist, the feeding

of the Five Thousand. The theological development has been
worked around the narratives or placed after them in the form of
obnoxious discourses. At this point in the book, however, the
pattern reverses itself, and theological reflection precedes the narratives. This may be an adaptation for what is to come, since the
discourses at the Last Supper, which interpret the passion and
resurrection, will best precede their narratives. The new order of
material is signaled by Jesus' proclamation of himself in 8:12 as
"the light of the cosmos," which points forward to the healing
of the man born blind, being echoed in 9:5.

5
ENLIGHTENMENT
(John 8:12—9:41)

Transition to this section of the
Gospel is critical for our author, for here he moves beyond the
external forms of membership in the Christian community and
deals with aspects of believing that have no clear or invariable
external indications. Enlightenment cannot be certified by fulfillment of a rite. What is more, it is not predictable, nor can it
be infallibly induced. It simply happens, and why it happens to
some and not to others remains a deep mystery. The discourses
of chapter 8 begin with an allusion to the images of light and dark
evoked in the prologue (1:4–5). This is not the topic of the chapter,
however, so much as it is one image for getting at something for
which human language has no standardized vocabulary: the fundamental unpredictability of human response. Why are some light
and some dark, some of the cosmos and others not, some from
above and some from below, some children of the great opponent,
Satan, and others children of God? The chapter does not resolve
the problem; it only insists on it.

(8:12) So Jesus again spoke to them, saying, "I am the light of the
cosmos. The person who follows me will never walk in the dark,
but will have the light of life." (13) So the Pharisees said to him,
"You're testifying about yourself; your testimony isn't true." (14)
Jesus answered and said to them, "Even if I should testify about
myself, my testimony is true because I know where I have come
from and where I am going. But *you* don't know where I am coming
from or where I am going. (15) *You* judge according to the flesh; *I*
don't judge anyone. (16) But even if I should judge, my judgment is
true, because it isn't just I, but I and the father who sent me. (17)
And even in your Law it's written that the testimony of two people

is true. (18) I am one testifying about myself and the father who sent me testifies about me." (19) So they said to him, "Where is your father?" Jesus answered, "You don't know me or my father. If you knew me, you would know my father, too." (20) He spoke these words in the treasure room, while teaching in the temple. And no one arrested him, because his hour had not yet come.

What Jesus says of himself here does not go much beyond what we read in the prologue: "In him there was life, and the life was the light of human beings" (1:4). The main difference is the association here with "following" Jesus. The life and light which were available in creation are now available in a new sense, overcoming the inexplicable alienation of cosmos from creator that has concerned John all along. The opponents of Jesus, however, confirm by their behavior that they are still caught in that alienation. They believe nothing of what he says and even contest his right to say it, for it seems that he is testifying about himself and he has already agreed (5:31) that self-testimony is false. Jesus appeals to the testimony of his father, but the opponents reply, "Where is he?" So far, they have only Jesus' word for what his father would say.

The opponents are right in a way; from their starting point, there is no way to understand or confirm what Jesus claims to be. On the other hand, their insistence on passing judgment in accordance with their own rules excludes them from real understanding in this matter. This is why Jesus here claims to judge no one, even though he said earlier (5:22) that the father had handed this function over to the son. There is a sense in which he really does not judge: he has no arbitrary rules to go by, for he is himself all original truth. He and the father are the source of all things, and there can be nothing arbitrary about their decisions.

The fact that Jesus' "hour" has not yet come is an indication of his supremacy and also of the impotence of his opponents. He will become vulnerable to them only when the divine will says that the hour has arrived. For now, he teaches not merely in the temple, but in the treasure room, which must surely have been heavily guarded and therefore an easy place to arrest him. Yet, nothing happens; and he taunts his opponents with their inability to get a grip on him:

(8:21) So he said again to them, "I'm going away and you will look for me; and you'll die in your sin. Where I'm going *you* cannot come." (22) So the Jews were saying, "Is he going to kill himself—since he's saying, 'Where I'm going you cannot come'?" (23) And he said to them, "*You* are from the realms below, *I* come from the realms above. *You* are from this cosmos, *I* am not from this cosmos. (24) I've told you, therefore, that you'll die in your sins; for if you don't believe that it is I, you'll die in your sins." (25) They said to him, then, "Just who are you?" Jesus said to them, "Whatever I'm telling you at the start![1] (26) I have many things to say about you and to judge. But the one who sent me is true, and I tell the cosmos these things that I've heard with him." (27) They did not know that he was telling them about the father. (28) So Jesus said, "Whenever you lift up the son of humanity, then you will know that it is I. And I do nothing on my own, but I say these things just the way the father has taught me. (29) And the one who sent me is with me; he hasn't left me alone, because I always do what pleases him." (30) As he was saying these things, many people believed in him.

The impasse is occasioned by Jesus' absolute priority in relation to the creation. The opponents will die "in their sins" if they don't believe him; yet, Jesus warns them of this precisely because they are from the wrong source, namely, the cosmos, the realms below. Does this make all belief impossible for them? No, but to overcome their disadvantage, they must reunderstand themselves and the cosmos as having their origin in the father through the logos. They will have to seek a new origin and a new identity, which is in fact their original reality, founded in Jesus himself. Yet, this turns out to be unthinkable for them, for they already see their origins and identity as if in a sacred light:

(8:31) So Jesus said to the Jews that had believed him, "If you stay in my word, you're really my disciples, (32) and you shall know the truth and the truth will set you free." (33) They replied to him, "We are seed of Abraham and have never been anyone's slaves. How can you say, 'You'll become free'?" (34) Jesus answered them, "Amen, amen, I say to you, everybody who commits sin is a slave. (35) And the slave doesn't stay in the household for ever; the son stays for ever. (36) So if the son sets you free, you will really be free. (37) I know that you are seed of Abraham; but you're trying to kill me, because my word doesn't find room in you. (38) I tell the things that I've seen with the father; you, too, then—do the things that you've heard of from the father!"

Communication has broken down entirely by this point. Jesus is speaking to a sympathetic group—Jews who have taken him seriously; yet, they cannot follow him. He speaks in riddling language about slavery and freedom. His hearers say, "We are freeborn"; Jesus says, "You are slaves by sin." His hearers say "father" and mean Abraham; Jesus says "father" and means God. The hearers cannot understand that there is anything of importance prior to Abraham or beyond their present, ambiguously sinful life. And their concern about their parentage, even though it was and is a legitimate aspect of God's dealing with humanity, becomes for them now a barrier against truth. Like the cosmos, religion itself comes from God, but becomes a sign of alienation. Accordingly it also becomes the object of Jesus' attacks:

(8:39) They replied and said to him, "Our father is Abraham." Jesus says to them, "If you were children of Abraham, you would be doing Abraham's works. (40) But as it is, you're trying to kill me, a person who has told you the truth that I've heard from God. This isn't what Abraham did. (41) You're doing your father's works, all right!" They told him, "We weren't born illegitimately; we have one father, God." (42) Jesus said to them, "If God were your father, you would love me, for I've come out from God and arrived here. For I didn't come on my own, either, but that one sent me. (43) Why don't you recognize what I say? Because you can't hear my word. (44) You're of your father the devil, and you're ready to act out your father's desires. That one was a killer from the start; and he didn't stand by the truth, because there's no truth in him. Whenever he tells the lie, he's speaking on his own, because he's a liar and so is his father. (45) But as for me—because I tell you the truth, you don't believe me. (46) Which of you is cross-examining me about sin? If I'm speaking truth, why don't you believe me? (47) The person who is from God hears God's words. This is why you don't hear—because you're not from God."

The question of fatherhood has now ceased to be a real question of descent: who is the devil's father, anyway? (This seems the most natural translation of v. 44.) He doesn't have one. It is simply a Semitic—and therefore biblical—way of expressing categories. The devil and the opponents belong to the category of "lie" and therefore cannot "hear" Jesus because he is speaking "truth," as is appropriate to his category ("being from God"). The irony is that Jesus is still, it seems, speaking to people who have believed him (v. 31). Yet, for the second time now he has accused them of trying to kill him. Ultimately, of course, it is a disciple who will betray him; but the accusation is proleptic even of the near future, for Jesus will shortly make them angry enough to commit mayhem on him.

(8:48) The Jews answered and said to him, "Aren't we right to say that you're a Samaritan and have a demon?" (49) Jesus replied, "I don't have a demon; but I'm honoring my father and you're dishon-

oring me. (50) But *I* don't look after my glory; there is someone who
looks after it and judges. (51) Amen, amen, I say to you, if anyone
keeps my word, he will never see death ever." (52) The Jews said to
him, "Now we know you have a demon. Abraham died and so did
the prophets; and *you* claim, 'If anyone keeps my word, he'll never
taste death ever'! (53) Are you more important than our father Abraham? He died! The prophets died, too! Whom do you make yourself?" (54) Jesus answered, "If I glorify myself, my glory is nothing.
It's my father who glorifies me—the one you claim is 'our God.' (55)
And you don't know him, but *I* know him. And if I should say that
I don't know him, I would be a liar like you. But I do know him and
I keep his word. (56) Abraham, your father, was glad to see my day;
and he saw it and was happy." (57) The Jews, then, said to him, "You
aren't fifty yet, and you've seen Abraham?!" (58) Jesus said to them,
"Amen, amen, I say to you, before Abraham came to be, I am." (59)
So they picked up rocks to throw at him, but Jesus hid himself and
left the temple.

It would be difficult to find a more depressing exchange in any
of the Gospels. This long, wrangling dialogue seems to demean
Jesus, especially when he gets caught in a childish flinging of
insults: You are children of the devil. . . . You have a demon. . . .
No, *I'm* not the one who has a demon. . . . Yes, you *do* have a
demon. . . . The two sides are now irreconcilable, especially from
v. 58 onward, for Jesus has used language there that is appropriate
only to God—not just the claim to antedate Abraham, but the
way he distinguishes himself, as simply "being," from Abraham,
who has "come to be." The teaching is in accord with the prologue; but it is utterly unacceptable to Jesus' audience, even
though they were described as "believers." They are now prepared
to inflict summary execution for blasphemy, and Jesus escapes
only narrowly.

Yet, it is just at this point of maximum alienation that we hear
of someone who was born blind (surely a citizen of the dark) who
nonetheless receives sight as a result of Jesus' ministry. The hope-
lessness of chapter 8 is not final. The world is not simply and
forever divided into God's children and the devil's, into above and
below, cosmos and not-cosmos, light and dark. The story that
now follows is told in very great detail, marking it as a focal point
in the whole Gospel:

(9:1) And as he was going along, he saw a person blind from birth.
(2) And his disciples asked him saying, "Rabbi, who sinned that this
man was born blind—he or his parents?" (3) Jesus answered, "Neither this man nor his parents sinned—but it was so that God's works

might be revealed in him. (4) We have to perform the works of the one that sent me while it is day; night is coming, when no one can do anything. (5) As long as I'm in the cosmos, I'm the light of the cosmos." (6) After saying these things, he spit on the ground and made mud with the spit, and anointed him with the mud on his eyes. (7) And he told him, "Go wash at the pool of Siloam" (which is translated "Sent"). So he went off and washed, and came back seeing. (8) So the neighbors and the people who used to observe him before (for he was a beggar) were saying, "Isn't this the man who used to sit and beg?" (9) Others said, "This is the one." Others said, "No, it's someone who looks like him." That man said, "It's I." (10) So they said to him, "How did your eyes get opened?" (11) That one answered, "The man called Jesus made mud and anointed my eyes and told me, 'Go to Siloam and wash.' So I went and washed and gained my sight." (12) And they said to him, "Where is that man?" He says, "I don't know."

Jesus' encounter with the blind man seems almost accidental. He has escaped from the temple, where he was threatened with violence, and his disciples (perhaps not the Twelve, as there has been no indication of their presence for some time now) interrupt their walk with a theological question. It would appear that the question might be of some interest to Jesus, who had earlier associated sin with sickness in the case of the paralytic at Bethzatha. There are several ways, in fact, in which this miracle echoes that of Bethzatha. Both take place at Jerusalem and involve a pool (John uses the unusual term *kolymbēthra* in both cases). In both narratives, Jesus performs the miracle without being asked. Both take place on Sabbath and therefore occasion conflict with the authorities. Yet, there is a major contrast in the mutual relation of three major elements: Jesus himself, sin, and the person healed.

At Bethzatha, Jesus warned the man against sin ("Stop sinning now, or something worse might happen to you," 5:14); but he promptly went to the authorities and betrayed Jesus. Here Jesus says that sin is not in question at all; this is simply an opportunity for God's works to be revealed in the blind man. And this man's response will prove to be one of dogged loyalty to his healer, even amidst adverse circumstances.[2] We might describe the relation between the two stories by saying that the Siloam washing reverses all that went wrong with that of Bethzatha. The difference lies in the absence of sin, for the man born blind, however much he belonged to the dark, does not refuse to see in Jesus the light of the world:

(9:13) They bring him to the Pharisees—the man who had been blind. (14) And it was Sabbath on the day when Jesus made the mud and opened his eyes. (15) So the Pharisees, too, questioned him again as to how he had gained his sight. And he said to them, "He put mud on my eyes, and I washed it off, and now I see." (16) So some of the Pharisees said, "This fellow is not from God, because he doesn't keep the Sabbath." But others said, "How can a sinful human being do such signs?" And there was a split among them. (17) So they say again to the blind man, "What do *you* say about him, since he opened *your* eyes?" And he said, "He's a prophet."

The authorities are still trying to deal with Jesus' actions in terms of a standard external to them: the Torah. The blind man must be interrogated because there has been a violation of one of the Ten Commandments. Some of his questioners are satisfied once they have determined that Jesus indeed performed work on the Sabbath. There is nothing ambiguous about the case, for he actually made a plaster and applied it, thus effecting healing by means of an "operation." Others, however, find themselves in conflict, for, though they take the Sabbath law with full seriousness, they are impressed by the miracle. Finding themselves at an impasse, the group even asks the (formerly) blind man for his opinion, which he gives without hesitation—"he's a prophet." (One recalls the Samaritan woman's similar confidence, 4:19, and the equal certainty of the crowds in 6:14 and 7:40.) The exchange is ironic, however, for a beggar who had been blind all his life cannot possibly know much about Torah—the principle the authorities are invoking. Whatever he says, they will not be able to take him seriously:

(9:18) The Jews, then, did not believe of him that he had been blind and had gained his sight, until they called the parents of the man who had gained his sight. (19) And they questioned them, saying, "Is this man your son? Do you declare that he was born blind? How, then, does he have sight now?" (20) So his parents answered and said, "We know that this is our son and that he was born blind. (21) But as to how he now sees, we don't know, or who opened his eyes *we* don't know. Question him. He's of age; *he'll* answer for himself." (22) His parents said these things because they were afraid of the Jews, for the Jews had already agreed that if anybody confessed him as anointed, he'd be excluded from the synagogue.[3] (23) This is why his parents said, "He's of age; question him."

This segment of the story suggests that the motive of the inquest is not just to establish that a crime was committed. (After all, Jesus has proven impossible to arrest thus far, anyway.) The objective now is to induce any possible witnesses to keep quiet, so that Jesus will get no credit for the event. The authorities are successful with the parents, but not with the blind man himself:

(9:24) So they called the man who had been blind back and told him, "Give God the glory! *We* know that this fellow is a sinner." (25) That man, then, replied, "Whether he's a sinner, I don't know. I know one thing—that though I was blind, I see now." (26) So they said to him, "What did he do to you? How did he open your eyes?" (27) He answered them, "I've told you already and you didn't listen. Why do you want to hear it again? Do *you* want to become disciples of his, too?" (28) And they abused him and said, "*You're* that fellow's disciple, but *we* are disciples of Moses. (29) We know that God spoke to Moses—but as for this man, we don't know where he's from." (30) The man responded and said to them, "Well, here's a wonder—you don't know where he's from; and he opened my eyes! (31) We know that God doesn't listen to sinners; but if anyone is reverent and does what he wants, this is the one he listens to! (32) From the beginning of time, it's never been heard of for anyone to open the eyes of a person born blind. (33) If this man weren't from God, he couldn't do anything." (34) They answered and said to him, "You were born altogether in sin, and are you teaching us?!" And they threw him out.

Had the authorities been content, on this round of questioning, with the man's first answer, all would have been well, for he carefully avoids saying more than the unavoidable minimum about the event and offers no appraisal of Jesus. The issue is entirely too awkward for them, however, and they cannot leave it alone. They are still looking for some bit of evidence that will relieve them of their own uncertainty about Jesus—in accordance, of course, with their prejudgments in the matter. Instead of finding that bit of evidence, they merely push the witness toward a more intransigent stance. It was one thing for him to agree to give God the glory; one could interpret that in various ways. But he will not cooperate with their effort to undermine the one who healed him, and when pressed he reacts angrily. At last, his own assessment of the event comes out: from the beginning of time there has been nothing like it (strong echo of the prologue) and it is therefore a world-shattering and a world-rebuilding event.

The point of the development is neatly encapsulated in the authorities' last words to the man: they accuse him of the sinfulness from which Jesus has already, so to speak, exonerated him. So it must always be. What is God's glory, seen from the angle of truth, must necessarily appear as sin, seen from the angle of falsehood. Their judgment is a judgment on them, as we shall see, since it is only a vindication of their own misunderstanding. From now on, Jesus is the standard for reverence and for doing the will of God; it is Torah that must give way. The man healed of blindness has recognized this; he looks to Jesus now as the one reliable point of access between God and humanity, as the touchstone of everything in human life. This moment of enlightenment is the great turning point of John's Gospel:

(9:35) Jesus heard that they had thrown him out, and he found him and said, "Do you believe in the son of humanity?" (36) That one answered and said, "Just who is he, sir, so that I may believe in him?" (37) Jesus said to him, "You've seen him, in fact, and the person talking with you is the one." (38) And he said, "I believe, sir." And he bowed down to him.

This is a curious exchange, but that is what is important about it. Jesus asks the man whether he believes in a certain figure that apparently means nothing to him. "Son of humanity" is a term Jesus has used here and there throughout the Gospel to refer to himself. He may have borrowed it from contemporary apocalyptic speculation about a humanlike redeemer; but since the evidence on the point is not altogether clear, scholars are still arguing the question. At any rate, in this story, the phrase "son of humanity" seems to mean nothing at all to the man. If he thought of it as a synonym of "messiah," for example, he could easily have said, "Yes, I believe he will come," much as the Samaritan woman expressed her faith (4:25). Instead, he is faced with a, to him, meaningless question. And his response is to say, "You tell me what to believe and I will believe." In other words, the man has placed total trust in Jesus as source of truth. And when Jesus identifies himself as this object of belief, the man does not hesitate to perform an act of reverence before him. This is the most adequate response to Jesus in the Gospel thus far, comparable only to the faith of Mary and of the royal official in the Cana miracles, yet going beyond them.[4]

The blind man's gaining of sight is thus a metaphor for his spiritual enlightenment, and John closes this portion of the Gospel with a complex proclamation by Jesus on this subject:

(9:39) And Jesus said, "It is for judgment that I've come into this cosmos, so that those who don't see may see and those who see may go blind." (40) Those of the Pharisees who were with him heard these things and said to him, "We aren't blind, too, are we?" (41) Jesus said to them, "If you were blind, you would have no sin. But, as it is, you claim that you see. Your sin is still there.

It is not only that one must move, somehow, from dark to light; there is an added complication in that people are inclined to confuse the two. It is easy to claim one's religious stance as light and not know that it is dark. After all, how does the person blind from birth know the difference? Since it is so hard to know one's true status, the wise course is to claim nothing for oneself. For unrecognized or unacknowledged blindness is the source and guarantee of sin.

True sight is to see things as they really are. That will not be easy, for we are caught in that desperate alienation from the creator which John described in the prologue as "the dark." We cannot see truly what we are afraid to see. The essence of the blind man's enlightenment was to recognize in Jesus the touchstone of reality. He does not, of course, express it in a full-fledged Johannine doctrine of the Christ, but in ways appropriate to the narrative. The drift, however, is the same. As long as one is oriented toward the son, one sees; turn toward some other standard of reality, and one is blind.

6
NEW LIFE
(John 10:1—12:19)

Enlightenment is not an end in itself. The prologue told us that the logos has given to some the right to become God's children. In his conversation with Nicodemus, Jesus spoke of both seeing and entering the reign of God. In both cases, the language suggests a new kind of existence. To see and know the real nature of our world in relation to its creator is essential to this new life, but not identical with it. As believer, one cannot remain content with knowledge, but must let this recognition of reality transform one's way of being. At first, this is not a transition which takes one out of this world (though that, too, will come); it is more nearly a change of allegiance.

In the present section of the Gospel of John, we have first a discourse centering on the metaphor of sheep and shepherd, then the narrative of the raising of Lazarus (with some associated events). The Lazarus story provides the same kind of compelling image for this section of the work that the healing of the man born blind did for the preceding one. The literary transition from Enlightenment to New Life, like that from Eucharist to Enlightenment, is signaled only by a change of subject matter, not by any seam in the narrative:

(10:1) "Amen, amen, I say to you, if a person doesn't enter the sheep-fold by the gate, but gets over the wall some other way, that person is a thief and robber. (2) But the one who goes in by the gate is shepherd of the sheep. (3) For this one, the gatekeeper opens up; and the sheep hear his voice, and he calls his own sheep by name and leads them out. (4) Once he gets all his own out, he walks ahead of them; and the sheep follow him because they know his voice. (5)

They won't follow a stranger; they'll run away from him because they don't know the stranger's voice."

The imagery of sheep and shepherd will have been familiar enough to ancient Mediterranean peoples, given the importance of sheep in the economy. The particular meaning associated with the imagery, however, could vary from one context to another. In Greek and Latin literature of the Hellenistic Age, the imagery generally evoked an idealized, uncomplicated country life as portrayed in pastoral poetry. The focus was often gently erotic. That does not appear to be the background here, however, even if it does affect our responses to this chapter because of the incorporation of such motifs into English poetry. It is more likely that the shepherd imagery here is royal imagery. "Shepherd" was a common synonym for "ruler" in the Jewish scriptures (it is also found in the Homeric epics of the Greeks). That is the meaning, for example, in "The Lord is my shepherd," which the ancient Latin translations correctly paraphrased as "Dominus regit me." Having recognized that Jesus is both the speaker and the touchstone of truth, one's next step is to place oneself under his direction, to know his voice and to follow him. This is how we signal our recognition of his legitimacy:

(10:6) Jesus told them this figure, but those people did not know what it was that he was telling them. (7) So Jesus said again, "Amen, amen, I say to you, *I* am the gate for the sheep. (8) All that have come are thieves and robbers, but the sheep haven't listened to them. (9) *I* am the gate. If anybody enters through me, he'll be safe and he'll go in and out and find pasture. (10) The thief only comes to steal and slaughter and destroy; I've come so that they may have life and have more even than they need.[1]

(11) "*I* am the good shepherd. The good shepherd lays down his life for the sheep. (12) When a person is a hired hand and not a real shepherd and the sheep aren't his own, he catches sight of the wolf coming and leaves the sheep and runs away (and the wolf grabs and scatters them) (13) because he's a hired hand and doesn't care about the sheep. (14) *I* am the good shepherd; and I know my own sheep and my own know me, (15) just the way the father knows me and I know the father. And I lay down my life for the sheep.

(16) "And I have other sheep who aren't of this fold. I have to bring those, too. And they will hear my voice, and there will come to be one flock, with one shepherd. (17) This is why the father loves me— because I'm laying down my life so that I may take it up again. (18) No one is taking it away from me, but I'm laying it down by my own choice. I have the right to lay it down, and I have the right to

take it up again. This is the commandment I've received from my father."

(19) A split developed again among the Jews because of these words. (20) Many of them were saying, "He has a demon and he's raving. Why are you listening to him?" (21) Others said, "These are not the words of a possessed person! Can a demon open blind people's eyes?"

The juxtaposition of metaphors in this speech does not so much clarify as deepen the imagery. Jesus is the gate—the only legitimate point of access; he is the good shepherd—the only true ruler; the sheep are really his—he is agent of creation; he and they know one another as intimately as he and his father; the sheep will listen to no one else; there are unsuspected sheep elsewhere to be brought into the one great flock. And all this at the expense of Jesus' own life. The life of the sheep, that is, will cost that of Jesus—not as a forced sacrifice but because Jesus, in the utter freedom of his power and in continuity with the father's loving command, has volunteered to do this.

The language is deliberately mysterious. There is no intention to clarify matters. Indeed, for the enlightened, there is now no need. Jesus is, in the last analysis, all there is for human beings. The believer relies on him for food and light and life—not the cosmic daily emblems of these things so much as the things themselves. The unenlightened, however, can make no sense of it all. Jesus' audience goes on fighting among themselves, and his opponents are still trying to find some external mode of verification that will settle for them who he is:

(10:22) The feast of the dedication came then at Jerusalem. It was winter. (23) And Jesus was walking in the temple in Solomon's portico. (24) So the Jews surrounded him and said to him, "How long are you going to hold our lives in suspense? If you are the anointed, tell us plainly." (25) Jesus answered them, "I've told you, and you don't believe. The works I'm doing in my father's name—these testify about me; (26) but you don't believe because you don't belong to my sheep. (27) My sheep listen to my voice; and I know them, and they follow me. (28) And I'm giving them everlasting life; and they'll never be destroyed ever, and no one will grab them out of my hand. (29) What my father has granted me is more important than everything put together, and no one can grab anything out of the father's hand. (30) I and the father are one."

This challenge by the authorities elicits from Jesus the ultimate statement of his identity: I and the father are one. The reader has been fully prepared for such a claim from the beginning of the book: "The logos was with God and the logos was God." The opponents, however, cannot accept—cannot even comprehend it. They do not belong to Jesus' sheep. Only the enlightened one will be able to grasp the reality of Jesus' being; the opponents still think of him as one factor among many, when in truth he is all there is. Even the father can scarcely be thought or spoken without at the same time thinking and speaking the son, for there is no access to the father, even in thought, except through the son. "I and the father are one."

This knowledge gives Jesus confidence that his opponents cannot do any real harm. They can no more deprive him of anything that belongs to him than they can deprive God. They do not see it quite this way.

(10:31) The Jews again picked up stones to stone him. (32) Jesus answered them, "I've shown you many good deeds from the father. Which of them is it you're stoning me for?" (33) The Jews answered him, "We're not stoning you for a good deed, but for blasphemy and because you, though you're a human being, are making yourself God." (34) Jesus answered them, "Isn't it written in your law, 'I have spoken; you are gods'? (35) If he called those to whom the word of God came 'gods' (and what is written cannot be undone), (36) do you accuse the one that the father hallowed and sent into the cosmos of blaspheming because I said, 'I'm God's son'? (37) If I don't do my father's works, don't believe me; (38) but if I do, even if you don't believe me, believe the works—so that you may know and understand that the father is in me and I in the father."

Jesus seems almost perplexed that "I and the father are one" should be taken as blasphemy. When he repeats the charge in v. 36, he claims to have said only, "I'm God's son." This is not, however, a moment of absent-mindedness—or a legal ploy—but a normal consequence of Johannine language. The logos/son is both identical to God and distinct from God. Accordingly, whether Jesus calls himself "son" or claims full unity with God or uses the formula "the father in me and I in the father," it all comes to the same thing. And the language is true not only of Jesus, though in the primary sense it is true only of him. It is applicable to any one deeply formed by the truth.

This is why Jesus can resort to the verse from Psalm 82 to prove his point.[2] I have translated it "*I* have spoken; you are gods" in order to bring out the basis of Jesus' interpretation. The emphatic *I* is God's reference to himself in addressing a certain group (John assumes that they are human). Since God has spoken, God's word

(*logos,* very likely a play on the use of the term in the prologue)
has come to these people. And what is the consequence of its
arrival? "You are gods."[3] The mere arrival of God's word makes
gods of human beings. How, then, can anyone complain about
Jesus' way of speaking about himself? This interpretation, however, is so much at variance with the presuppositions of the opponents that they do not even do battle with it; they simply return
to their posture of active hostility:

(10:39) They were trying again to arrest him, and he escaped their
grasp. (40) And he went off again across the Jordan to the spot where
John had been at first, baptizing; and he stayed there. (41) And many
people came to him and were saying, "John didn't do a single sign,
but all the things John said about this man were true." (42) And
many people believed in him there.

Jesus' escape is a purely miraculous one, for the opponents had
had him surrounded during this argument (10:24). It is prudent
now to withdraw to the countryside. None of this slows down
the spread of Jesus' reputation, however, and he therefore remains
an object of suspicion. For him to return to the neighborhood of
Jerusalem is dangerous; yet, he will do just that to work his great-
est sign under his opponents' noses. In the shepherd discourse,
he had stressed his power to give and preserve life for his sheep.
He was talking then about a reorientation of all life, conditioned
by the knowledge of who he truly is. The language also had overtones, however, of the final resurrection from the dead which
many faithful Jews of Jesus' days expected (for example, one notes
the curious phrases about "laying down" life and "taking it up").
The raising of Lazarus, which now follows, comprehends both
aspects of life in a single image:

(11:1) Now, there was a certain sick man, Lazarus of Bethany, from
the village of Mary and her sister Martha. (2) (It was Mary that
anointed the lord with myrrh and wiped his feet with her hair—her
brother Lazarus was sick.) (3) So the sisters sent him a message,
saying, "Sir, look, the man you love is sick." (4) When Jesus heard,
he said, "This sickness is not for death but for the sake of God's
glory, so that God's son may be glorified through it." (5) Now Jesus
loved Martha and her sister and Lazarus. (6) So when he heard that
he was sick, at that time he stayed where he was two days. (7) Then
afterward he says to the disciples, "Let's go back to Judea." (8) The
disciples say to him, "Rabbi, just now the Jews were trying to stone
you—and you're going there again?" (9) Jesus replied, "Aren't there
twelve hours in the day? If somebody goes walking by day, he won't
stumble, because he sees the light of this cosmos. (10) But if anyone

walks by night, he does stumble because the light isn't in him." (11)
He said these things and afterward he says to them, "Our friend
Lazarus has fallen asleep, but I'm going so that I can wake him up."
(12) So the disciples said to him, "Sir, if he's fallen asleep, he'll be
all right." (13) (Now, Jesus had spoken about his death, but those
people supposed he was talking about ordinary sleep.) (14) So then
Jesus told them plainly, "Lazarus has died. (15) And I'm glad for your
sakes that I wasn't there—so that you may believe. But let's go to
him." (16) So Thomas, called "the twin," said to his fellow disciples,
"Let's go with him, too, so that we can die with him."

The beginning of this story is curiously halting. One would
never guess from the first sentence that Lazarus was related to
Mary and Martha. For that matter, we've never met the two sisters in this Gospel, and John identifies them by an incident (the
anointing) that will not happen until chapter 12. (Clearly, the
audience of the work is expected to know a good deal already
about the traditions of Jesus' life. This is not a work of reportage
so much as of interpretation.) Then, when Jesus receives the message about Lazarus' illness, he delays for two days before abruptly
announcing a return to the dangerous vicinity of Jerusalem. When
the disciples object, Jesus makes a cryptic remark about light
(though, in fact, it is cryptic only to those in the dark, for it means
that those who have the true light of the cosmos in themselves
cannot go wrong). Finally, when he does reveal that his mission
has to do with Lazarus, he does so in a misleading way.

"Lazarus has fallen asleep." Sleep and death are often images
of each other. Paul uses such terminology, for example, in 1 Cor.
15:20: "Now Christ has been raised from the dead, the first fruits
of those who have fallen asleep." There is no difficulty in understanding the metaphor except that it is used here without
warning. What is more, it does not occur to the disciples that
Lazarus's *death* might be a reason for Jesus to go to Bethany. He
might go there to heal the sick man, yes, but what can one do
for the dead?[4] To quote Paul again, "The last enemy to be defeated
is death" (1 Cor. 15:26).

(11:17) So when Jesus came, he found him in the tomb, already four
days dead. (18) Now, Bethany was close to Jerusalem, a couple of
miles away; (19) and many of the Jews had come to Martha and Mary
to console them for their brother. (20) So Martha, when she heard
Jesus was coming, went to meet him, but Mary kept her seat in the
house. (21) Martha, then, said to Jesus, "Sir, if you'd been here, my
brother wouldn't have died. (22) Even now I know that whatever you
ask God, God will give you." (23) Jesus says to her, "Your brother

will rise." (24) Martha says to him, "I know that he'll rise in the resurrection at the last day." (25) Jesus said to her, "*I* am the resurrection and the life. The one who believes in me, even if he dies, will live; (26) and everyone who lives and believes in me will never die to all eternity. Do you believe this?" (27) She says to him, "Yes, sir. I have believed that you are the anointed, God's son, the one coming into the cosmos."

Martha's conversation with Jesus affirms what the disciples, too, must have felt—that Jesus could have kept Lazarus from dying. But she also goes further, albeit in the allusive style of the Cana miracles: "Even now I know that whatever you ask God, God will give you." Yet, she is less than clear about the matter. When Jesus promises that her brother will rise, she thinks at once of the general resurrection in the last day, and she assumes that this can only be far off. Jesus responds with another of the emphatic "*I* am" sayings, declaring that the end of all things is as much under his authority as the beginning. "In him there was life" (1:4); "*I* am the resurrection and the life" (11:25). Martha acknowledges that this agrees with what she has believed all along. The power and authority of Jesus are such that he *is* life—and no one associated with him can possibly be deprived of what he is. Death may seem to supervene, but it is not the ultimate reality.

(11:28) And after saying these things, she went off and called her sister Mary privately, saying, "The teacher is here and he's calling you." (29) That woman, once she heard, got up quickly and came to him. (30) (Now, Jesus had not yet come into the village, but was still at the spot where Martha had met him.) (31) So the Jews who were with her in the house consoling her, when they saw that Mary got up quickly and left, followed her, supposing that she was going to the tomb to weep there. (32) So when Mary got to where Jesus was, once she saw him, she fell at his feet, saying to him, "Sir, if you'd been here, my brother wouldn't have died." (33) So when Jesus saw her crying and the Jews who'd come with her crying, he got angry in the spirit and grew disturbed; (34) and he said, "Where have you put him?" They say to him, "Sir, come and see." (35) Jesus wept. (36) So the Jews said, "See how he loved him!" (37) And some of them said, "Couldn't this man who opened the blind man's eyes also have kept this man from dying?"

There is excellent reason, from a prudential point of view, to keep Jesus' arrival secret; but it cannot be—and, in a higher sense, makes no difference. Jesus *is* life; no one can take life from him, though he is free to lay it down (10:18). Yet, his reaction to death

seems fully human. He grows angry at the weeping of the others—
not angry because of it, but because their outpouring of grief trig-
gers his own. He is not at this moment a figure of power or of
mystery; and one cannot be surprised if the bystanders speculate
about what he could have done had he come earlier, while never
thinking of what he might do now.

> (11:38) So Jesus, again growing angry inwardly, comes to the tomb.
> (It was a cave and a stone closed it.) (39) Jesus says, "Take the stone
> away." Martha, the sister of the deceased, says to him, "Sir, he stinks
> by now; for he's been dead four days." (40) Jesus says to her, "Didn't
> I tell you that, if you believe, you would see God's glory?" (41) So
> they took the stone away. And Jesus raised his eyes upward and said,
> "Father, I thank you for having heard me. (42) And *I* know that you
> always listen to me; but I've spoken for the sake of the crowd stand-
> ing around, so that they may believe that *you've* sent me." (43) And
> after saying these things, he shouted in a loud voice, "Lazarus, come
> out." (44) The dead man came out, tied foot and hand with strips of
> cloth, and his face was swathed in a handkerchief. Jesus tells them,
> "Untie him and let him go."

The narrative speaks for itself, and one can add nothing to its
awesome and frightening quality. The trappings of death still
cling to Lazarus as he struggles to the opening of the cave. Yet,
Jesus has fulfilled his promises: he has called his own by name
(10:3); he is the gate by which Lazarus reenters the world of the
living; he is the good shepherd who protects the flock from the
wolf; he is the resurrection and the life. But he has already warned
that this gift is given at the price of his own life, and the consequences of the miracle ensure that that will indeed be so:

> (11:45) So many of the Jews who had come to visit Mary and saw
> what he did believed in him, (46) but some of them went off to the
> Pharisees and told them what Jesus had done. (47) So the chief priests
> and Pharisees convened a Council meeting, and they were saying,
> "What do we do, since this fellow is doing many signs? (48) If we
> let him go on this way, all the people will believe in him, and the
> Romans will come and take away both our place and our nation."
> (49) But one of them, Caiaphas, who was high priest that year, said
> to them, "You don't know anything, (50) and you fail to reckon up
> that it's to your advantage that one person should die for the people
> and the whole nation not be destroyed." (51) Now, he did not say
> this on his own; but as he was high priest that year, he prophesied
> that Jesus would die for the nation—(52) and not only for the nation,
> but also so that the scattered children of God might be gathered into
> one. (53) So from that day on, they planned together to kill him. (54)
> So Jesus no longer walked around publicly among the Jews, but went

off from there to the countryside close to the wasteland, to a city
called Ephraim. And he spent some time there with his disciples.

The new life of Lazarus leads directly to Jesus' death, partly as
a result of political calculation. The Jewish authorities, after all,
were completely subordinate to the occupying power of the Romans. Like any native rulers under such circumstances, they
tended to keep one eye constantly focused on their overlords.
Mass movements were likely to make the Romans nervous and
might well result in the desolation of the temple ("our place")
and the virtual destruction of the Jewish nation in Palestine. In
66–70 C.E., a Jewish revolt against Rome resulted in consequences
like these, as did a second one in 132–35. John's Gospel was probably written between these two wars. Caiaphas, the high priest
and a well-tried politician, had the appropriate solution from the
point of view of *Realpolitik:* Jesus must be put out of the way.[5]

Such machinations, however, cannot really touch the Jesus of
John's Gospel. He has repeatedly and miraculously evaded arrest.
If the plot against him works now, it is because it is a part of the
divine will and Caiaphas has unwittingly spoken as prophet, not
as Roman puppet. As prophets often do, he said more than he
knew. Jesus' death will benefit not only the nation of Israel, but
all of God's scattered children. One hears an echo of Jesus' earlier
language: "I have other sheep who aren't of this fold. I have to
bring those, too." John never says exactly who these other sheep
are. They may be Diaspora Jews or even Gentiles. At any rate,
what distinguishes all of them is that they are "God's scattered
children"—those to whom Jesus has given power to become such
(1:12–13).

By his death, he will gather them "into one." The expression
in Greek may mean no more than "together." On the other hand,
it has in it an echo of Jesus' outrageous claim "I and the father
are one" (10:30). The word "one" in Greek is, in both cases, *hen*—
literally, "one thing"—not *hena*, "one person," as one might have
expected in chapter 10. The oddness of the neuter gender in the
former passage sticks in the mind and gives a slight emphasis to
the same word in the present passage. That this is in fact no
accident will emerge more clearly in our discussion of chapter
17.

Jesus once again retreats to safer territory, but not now so far
away as previously. The stage is set for a final journey to the
capital and a climactic confrontation with the opponents:

(11:55) Now, the Jews' passover was soon, and many people went up to Jerusalem from the countryside before passover to purify themselves. (56) So they were looking for Jesus and saying to each other as they stood in the temple, "What do you think? He'll never come to the feast, will he?" (57) But the chief priests and the Pharisees had given orders, if any one knew his whereabouts, to tell, so that they could arrest him. (12:1) So Jesus came, six days before the feast, to Bethany, where Lazarus was, whom Jesus had raised from the dead. (2) So they had a dinner for him there; and Martha was serving, but Lazarus was one of those at table with him. (3) So Mary took twelve ounces of valuable perfume, nard in a pistachio-oil base, and anointed Jesus' feet and wiped his feet with her hair. And the house was filled with the fragrance of the perfume. (4) But Judas the Iscariot, one of his disciples, the one who would betray him, says, (5) "Why hasn't this perfume been sold for three hundred denarii and given to the poor?" (6) (Now, he said this not because he cared about the poor, but because he was a thief and, since he held the purse, he would take what was put in.) (7) So Jesus said, "Let her be—to keep it for the day of my entombment. (8) For you always have the poor with you, but you don't always have me." (9) So a great crowd of the Jews knew he was there; and they came not on Jesus' account only but also to see Lazarus, whom he had raised from the dead. (10) And the chief priests planned together to kill Lazarus, too, (11) because many of the Jews went on account of him and believed in Jesus.

The situation is very dangerous, but the family at Bethany risks Jesus' presence. They are like the man born blind in terms of their loyalty—and a great contrast to the paralytic or to Judas. At the dinner they give for Jesus, Lazarus, instead of being one of the hosts, has the place of an honored guest. Indeed, he is as great an attraction now as the man who raised him. So tightly is his life now wedded to that of Jesus, that those who are planning the death of the one must now also plan the death of the other.

At the dinner itself, Mary performs an extravagant act of homage to Jesus, not only by anointing him with enormously expensive perfume, but by demeaning herself to wipe his feet with her own hair. (This striking behavior was enough to identify her to the original Johannine audience, 11:2.) It is hard for the modern reader to disentangle John's version of the story from those in Matthew and Mark or from the related narrative in Luke.[6] What John stresses is, first, the extravagance of the action, which makes it memorable; second, the objection of Judas, which both underlines the value of the perfume and also affords an opportunity to contrast his own falseness with the loyalty of Mary; and, finally, that the remainder of the perfume is to be kept for Jesus' entombment. Matthew and Mark, by contrast, assume that all the perfume was used up and that this was itself the "anointing for burial." If, in John's Gospel, this is not the anointing for burial, what is it? Perhaps simply an act of worship, like the blind man's prostration (9:38), or perhaps another kind of anointing. In ancient Israel, kings, priests, and occasionally prophets entered upon their office through anointing; indeed, that is the sense of the title "messiah" or "christ"—"anointed one." Perhaps, then, this is an irregular kind of royal anointing; certainly, it is followed at once by a royal entry into the capital. But, of course, we remember that the shepherd-king is one who lays down his life for his sheep; the oil of consecration may readily become that of burial as well.

(12:12) The next day, the big crowd that had come for the feast, having heard that Jesus was coming into Jerusalem, (13) got palm branches and went out to meet him. And they were shouting, "Hosanna! Blessed be the one who comes in the Lord's name, and blessed be the king of Israel." (14) And Jesus found a little ass and sat on it, just as it stands written: (15) "Don't be afraid, daughter of Zion! See, your king is coming, sitting on an ass's foal." (16) His disciples did not recognize these things at first; but when Jesus had been glorified, then they remembered that these things had been written about him and that they had done these things for him. (17) So the crowd that was with him when he called Lazarus out of the tomb and raised him from the dead testified. (18) This is the reason, too, that the crowd came to meet him—because they heard that he had done this sign. (19) So the Pharisees said to each other, "You see that you've been accomplishing nothing! Look, the cosmos has gone off after him."

Jesus' triumphal entry (palm branches were symbols of victory) means that the people recognize him as king. Yet, it is a miracle, the raising of Lazarus, that evokes this upwelling of popular sentiment. The two may seem unrelated, but in fact are not. This section of the Gospel began with the shepherd discourse, where Jesus bases his kingly claims on the care that he takes for his own. The raising of Lazarus is a supreme expression of that care—and therefore the vindication of his royalty. To enter God's reign has been one way of stating the goal of this whole journey through conversion, Baptism, Eucharist, and enlightenment. To have everlasting life, resurrection life, is another image for that goal. In John's account of the triumphal entry, both images are brought together.

And Jesus' work does seem like a success. Perhaps the opponents are overstating matters when they claim that "the cosmos
has gone off after him." There are still plenty of enemies left; the
dark is still well populated. Yet, there is a measure of truth in
what they say. More of the cosmos than meets the eye is being
drawn to Jesus and it will radically affect the mode of his mission
in the next section of the Gospel. New life is achieved for those
who belong to Jesus. It is time to pay life for life.

7
UNION I
(John 12:20—13:30)

More than once, in John's Gospel, we have heard Jesus' activity or the events affecting him explained by the fact that his "hour" (*hōra*) or "time" (*kairos*) had not yet come. Jesus uses this explanation with his mother at Cana (2:4) and again with his brothers when they urge him to go up and work miracles in Jerusalem during the feast of Tabernacles (7:6). John also resorts to it twice to explain why efforts to arrest Jesus failed (7:30; 8:20). Now, a seemingly minor incident persuades Jesus that the hour *has* come, and the reader must prepare for the pace and direction of the work to change.

> (12:20) Now, there were some Greeks among those who were coming up to worship at the feast. (21) So these people approached Philip, who was from Bethsaida in Galilee, and asked him, saying, "Sir, we want to see Jesus." (22) Philip comes and tells Andrew; Andrew comes with Philip and they tell Jesus. (23) And Jesus answers them, saying, "The hour has come for the son of humanity to be glorified. (24) Amen, amen, I say to you, unless the grain of wheat, once it has fallen into the earth, dies, it remains alone; but if it dies, it produces a great yield. (25) The person who loves his life loses it, and the person who hates his life in this cosmos will protect it into everlasting life. (26) If anybody is serving me, let him follow me; and where I am, there my servant will be, too. If anybody serves me, the father will honor him.

It is not immediately obvious who the "Greeks" are, whose request signals the arrival of the "hour," for the word might refer either to gentile sympathizers of Judaism or to Greek-speaking Jews. In Paul's writings and in Acts, the term *Hellēnes* ("Greeks") usually refers to Gentiles; in Acts, Luke occasionally uses a specialized term (the related *Hellēnistai*) to denote Greek-speaking Jews. Johannine usage, however, has only the single term. Thus, in 7:35, the opponents wondered whether Jesus was planning "to go into the diaspora of the Greeks and teach the Greeks." Their language implies Greek-speaking Jews, not Gentiles. In the present passage, too, the "Greeks" are part of the crowds that have come to Jerusalem to worship (literally, "prostrate themselves," as the blind man did before Jesus in 9:38) at the feast. It is most likely, then, that they are Greek-speaking Jews who, unlike Gentiles, could take full part in the solemnities.[1]

The implication of the story is that Jesus' ministry has hitherto been exclusively within the Aramaic- and Hebrew-speaking segment of the populace. Speakers of Greek had no direct way to approach him; therefore they sought out a disciple who came from a bilingual city, Bethsaida-Julias, and who had a Greek name. This one, Philip, sought help from another disciple with a Greek name, Andrew, who was also from Bethsaida, as we were pointedly told quite early on, in 1:44. The two went together to Jesus, and Jesus responded with his dramatic exclamation, "The hour has come!"

How can the request of a few Greek-speaking Jews make such a difference? For it is merely their request, not any actual meeting with them, that is in question; in fact, we never find out whether Jesus grants them an audience or not. Either John has been remarkably clumsy in this regard, or else he has left some less obvious clue somewhere in the book as to the importance he attached to this incident. Perhaps we find such an indication in the shepherd discourse: "And I have other sheep who aren't of this fold. I have to bring those, too. And they will hear my voice, and there will come to be one flock, one shepherd" (10:16). The phrase "I have to bring" is a very strong one in Greek, of a type often used in apocalyptic language to say that an event is a necessary and unavoidable consequence of God's will. The fulfillment of this expectation, then, could readily figure as a key indicator of the "time," telling precisely where one is in the divinely willed sequence of events.

Still, the event itself hardly seems very important. While we know little about relations between Greek- and Semitic-speaking Jews in the first century, any division or antagonism that might have existed between the two language groups was surely minimal compared, for example, to the hatred between Jews and Samaritans, overcome already in chapter 4. What is important in

this case, however, is not the general question of relations between the two groups, but the fact that the Johannine literature
is written in Greek. The Johannine communities somehow identified these enquiring Greeks as their own emergent nucleus. Despite the fact that they did not belong to the original following
of Jesus ("are not of this fold"), Jesus has called them, too, and
they have come.[2]

Their appearance clears the way for Jesus' death, which will
bear fruit in new life for his followers. It will be a paradoxical
life. Indeed, their new life may involve death in terms of this
cosmos, just as Jesus himself was doomed by his giving of life to
Lazarus. Yet, this is the passage into unity: "one flock, one shepherd" . . . "where I am, there my servant will be, too."

> (12:27) "Now my soul is disturbed. And what am I to say? 'Father,
> save me from this hour'? But this is why I've come to this hour. (28)
> Father, glorify your name." So a voice came from heaven, "I have
> glorified it and I shall glorify it again." (29) So the crowd that was
> standing and listening said it had thundered. Others were saying,
> "An angel has spoken to him." (30) Jesus answered and said, "This
> voice didn't come for my sake, but for yours. (31) Now is the judg-
> ment of this cosmos; now the ruler of this cosmos will be thrown
> out. (32) And I—if I am lifted up from the earth, I shall draw all
> people to myself." (33) (Now, he was saying this to indicate what
> kind of death he would die.) (34) So the crowd answered him, "We've
> heard from the law that the anointed stays for ever. How can *you*
> say that the son of humanity has to be lifted up? Who is this 'son
> of humanity'?" (35) So Jesus said to them, "The light is with you a
> little while yet. Walk while you have the light, so that the darkness
> won't overtake you. And the person walking in the darkness doesn't
> know where he's going. (36) While you have the light, believe in the
> light, so that you may become children of light." Jesus said these
> things and left and hid himself from them.

Jesus' human anxiety about death, evident in his weeping over
Lazarus, appears again here in the form of a debate with himself
about how to pray. His "hour" involves his death; he would like
to pray to be delivered from that. Instead, he substitutes another
prayer: "Father, glorify your name." Thus he acknowledges God's
absolute primacy, which is the source of all that he is; and God
responds. His death plays an essential part in God's work—it will
be the means of drawing all people to Jesus. (Perhaps even Gentiles are in view at this point, though it is impossible to be sure.)
It also signals the deposition of this world's ruler and, thus, the
succession of a new reign. As Jesus is the gate of the sheepfold

and the resurrection and the life, so is his death the door to the world to come.

The crowd protests that, if he is messiah, he cannot go away; he most particularly cannot die a violent death. Later on, Jesus will elaborate on the reasons why he must leave; for now, he merely reaffirms his departure. Interestingly, he goes back to light imagery in doing so. We begin to look back along the road we have traversed in the previous chapters. Jesus' words in vv. 23–28 emphasized the theme of life; now, in vv. 35–50, he returns to the earlier theme of light. (This retrospective movement will continue in chapter 13.) The light will not be here much longer, he says; once it is gone, you cannot find your way. And then he who is himself that light disappears.

The voice of John breaks in again now to interpret:[3]

(12:37) Now, even though he had done such signs in their presence, they did not believe in him, (38) so that what the prophet Isaiah said might be fulfilled: "Lord, who has believed our report? And to whom has the Lord's arm been revealed?" (39) This is why they could not believe, because, again, Isaiah said: (40) "It has blinded their eyes and hardened their hearts, so that they should not see with the eyes and understand with the heart and turn back—and I should heal them." (41) Isaiah said these things because he saw his glory and spoke of him. (42) And yet, even from among the Council members, many believed in him; but they would not admit it on account of the Pharisees, so that they would not be excluded from the synagogue. (43) For they loved the glory that comes from human beings more than the glory from God.

John, like other early Christians, was deeply perplexed by the failure of the people to understand all that Jesus signified. He takes refuge in the recognition that it was the same with the prophets: Isaiah, too, could proclaim God's power (metaphorically, God's arm) and not be believed. But why? One might speak of a kind of inhibition of eye and heart and mind (for "heart," in this idiom, refers to what we would call both "heart" and "mind"). This implies that the people were unable to respond—a conclusion already suggested in the prologue and in such sayings as 10:26: "But you don't believe because you don't belong to my sheep." Some people are blind, even though they claim to see (9:39–41).

Ultimately, one must simply admit, as the prologue does, that even though the cosmos stems entirely from God's act of creation in and through the logos, it is now alienated from its creator.

When God's glory is revealed, it seems that the cosmos should naturally turn back toward it. And it has been revealed: we have beheld it, says the prologue (1:14). Long before, Isaiah had had a vision of it; and at this instant the voice from heaven has just declared, "I have glorified my name and I will glorify it." But the cosmos refuses to turn back, nonetheless, and the glory of human beings blinds people to the glory of God.

That is why Jesus is essential, for John. To be initiated into him, to be enlightened and brought to new life in him, turns one away from the standards of this world and replaces them with truth, with an acknowledgment that only God is ultimately true or real and that everything else is derivative.

> (12:44) And Jesus shouted and said, "The one who believes in me doesn't believe in me, but in the one that sent me; (45) and the one who sees me sees the one that sent me. (46) I have come into the cosmos as light, so that everyone that believes in me won't remain in the dark. (47) And if someone hears my words and doesn't keep them, I don't judge him; for I didn't come to judge the cosmos, but to save the cosmos. (48) The one who ignores me and doesn't accept my words (rhēmata) has one to judge him: the word (logos) that I've spoken, that will judge him on the last day. (49) For I have not spoken on my own, but the father who sent me—he has given me a command what to say and what to speak. (50) And I know that his command is everlasting life. So, then, the things I speak, I speak just the way the father told me."

Jesus is transparent to God: belief in Jesus is belief in God; to look at Jesus is to see God. This is the realization of what was said in the prologue: "As for God, no one has ever seen him; the only-child God, the one who is in the father's bosom—that one has explained" (1:18). Jesus does not do this in order to judge human beings; and yet, judgment is the inescapable result. There can be no further doubt whether one has turned to the father or not, for there is a clear standard: the logos of the logos, the word of God's word. This is all the light and all the truth—and all the access to God—there is.

John comes now, in his narrative, to Jesus' Last Supper with his disciples; but he treats the story in a way quite different from our other sources.[4] He gives no narrative of the institution of the Lord's Supper or Eucharist; rather, the meal becomes the setting for two long discourses and a prayer, which interpret Jesus' departure. This does not mean that John is uninterested in the Lord's Supper; only that he has shifted his treatment of it to another point in the book (chapter 6). In fact, the complete rite of Christian initiation, Baptism and Eucharist together, enters into the present narrative through verbal and symbolic echoes. (This continues the reprise of earlier themes in reverse order, noted above.) John has placed the dinner one full day of the month earlier than the Synoptics; for him, it is not the passover meal, but a private supper preceding passover:[5]

> (13:1) Before the feast of the passover, Jesus knew that his hour had come for him to cross over from this cosmos to the father; having loved his own who were in the cosmos, he loved them to the end. (2) And when supper was under way (the devil had already prompted Judas, son of Simon Iscariot, to betray him), (3) knowing that God had put all things into his hands and that he had come from God and was going to God, (4) he gets up from supper and takes off his clothes and took a linen towel and tied it around his waist. (5) Then he puts water into the basin and began to wash the disciples' feet and dry them with the towel that was around his waist. (6) So he comes to Simon Peter. He says to him, "Sir, are *you* going to wash *my* feet?" (7) Jesus answered and said to him, "You don't know now what I'm doing, but you will come to know later on." (8) Peter says to him, "You'll never wash my feet—to all eternity!" Jesus answered him, "If I don't wash you, you have no share with me." (9) Simon Peter says to him, "Sir, not just my feet, but my hands and my head, too." (10) Jesus says to him, "The person who's bathed doesn't need to wash, except for the feet, but is clean all over. And you people are clean—but not all of you." (11) For he knew his betrayer. This is why he said, "You're not all clean."

John interprets for us the significance of "the hour"—not only this moment at the Last Supper, but the whole of the passion, death, and resurrection. It is the hour for Jesus "to cross over from this cosmos to the father." All things are in Jesus' power; he has received all (even his own being) from the father and is returning with all to the father. Yet, he does not thereby deprive this cosmos of its being. It still exists and is still in the state described in the prologue—utterly derivative and dependent, and yet alienated from its creator. It is the same cosmos as before and the son still has in it those who are "his own."

This is not some guarantee of the goodness or enlightenment of these people. As the prologue said, "He came to what is his own, and those who are his own did not receive him" (1:11). This is still true. The principal betrayer is at the supper alongside all the lesser betrayers. What is more, he is already inwardly launched on his course of betrayal, and Jesus knows this. Still, "having loved his own who were in the cosmos, he loved them to the end." (One might also translate, "to the full.") He expresses this love in a servant's act, the washing of their feet; and when Peter, acutely and understandably embarrassed, protests, he insists that this is the only way to be a partner with him. One *must* be served by him—indeed, cannot escape it, since he is life and light and resurrection and gate. There is no being of any kind without him.

Service, however, is not the only issue; cleansing is another. Feet get dusty from the road and have to be washed repeatedly. Yet, this is not a complete bath; the implication is that the disciples have had that. Now, Jesus is simply tidying them up. It is easy here, though not unavoidable, to see an allusion to baptism. John has spoken of baptism previously as rebirth and as the quenching of thirst; but the idea of baptism as a bath was also familiar within first-century Christianity.[6] If footwashing was a regular rite in the Johannine communities, it could easily have been understood as a harking back to baptism and might even have played a role in the forgiveness of postbaptismal sin. Since the disciples have been baptized, they do not need another complete bath.

And yet, as John hinted before, the external rites, however essential, guarantee nothing. "You people are clean—but not all of you." This is not to suggest that Judas had somehow escaped being baptized like the rest. His uncleanness consists of his forthcoming betrayal of Jesus. To a lesser degree, most of the disciples will betray Jesus. There are no guarantees of human constancy: "His own did not receive him."

What Jesus has done has a further significance; it sets a pattern not only for the disciples' relationship to him, but for their relationship with one another.

(13:12) So when he had washed their feet, he put his clothes on and took his place at table again. He said to them, "Do you recognize what I've done for you? (13) *You* call me 'The Teacher' and 'The Lord'; and you're right to say so, for I am. (14) So if I, the lord and the teacher, have washed your feet, you should wash each other's feet, too. (15) For I've given you an example, so that you, too, will do just as I've done for you. (16) Amen, amen, I say to you, a slave is not greater than his lord and an agent is not greater than the one who sent him. (17) If you know these things, you are blessed—if you do them. (18) I'm not talking about all of you; I know whom I chose! But it was so that what is written might be fulfilled: 'The person that chews my bread has raised his heel against me.' (19) From now on, I'm telling you before it happens, so that you'll believe, whenever it does happen, that I am he. (20) Amen, amen, I say to you, the one who receives anyone I send receives me, and the one who receives me receives the one that sent me."

Jesus' discourse hints of things to come. He says that the disciples must imitate his example, to begin with, because they are his inferiors: his slaves and agents. (The Greek word for "agent" here is *apostolos*, "apostle." John does not use it elsewhere, nor does he treat it as an official designation for the Twelve or for any other early Christian group. He may well, however, have expected his audience to associate it with specific individuals such as Peter.) Yet, just as Jesus is transparent to the father, so Jesus' agents are transparent to Jesus. Thus, he brings the disciples into a kind of union with himself and God that will be explored more fully later on.

One cannot say whether the original Johannine audience would have understood Jesus to be instituting footwashing as a rite or whether they would have taken the passage solely as metaphor or acted prophecy. This would depend on the liturgical usage they were familiar with, and that is lost to us.[7] In either case, however, the humble and forgiving stance of Jesus is made the model for relationships within the church. Blessed are those who not only know this, but do it! There are those who, even with all the advantages of the disciples, still fail.[8] Jesus chose Judas. He has been baptized into the community, had his feet washed by Jesus, and eaten Jesus' bread. Yet, he is not a recipient of the blessing. In chapter 6, it seemed as if chewing Jesus' flesh might give some assurance of life; but now it appears that even the bread of the Last Supper offers no such hope. "The person that chews my bread has raised his heel against me."[9]

The failure of Baptism and Eucharist also implies, as we move back one step further, a failure of conversion. Indeed, there takes place a kind of retro-conversion, which takes Judas away from all that Jesus represents:[10]

(13:21) After saying these things, Jesus became disturbed in the spirit and testified and said, "Amen, amen, I say to you, one of you will betray me." (22) The disciples were looking at one another, at a loss as to whom he meant. (23) One of his disciples, whom Jesus loved, was lying at Jesus' breast; (24) so Simon Peter signals him to enquire who it might be he was speaking of. (25) So that man, lying as he was at Jesus' breast, says to him, "Sir, who is it?" (26) Jesus answers,

"It's that one for whom I'll sop the piece of bread and give it to him."
So, after soaking the piece of bread, he takes and gives it to Judas,
son of Simon Iscariot. (27) And after the bread then Satan entered
that man. So Jesus says to him, "What you're doing, do right away."
(28) None of those at table knew why he said this, (29) for some
supposed (since Judas held the purse) that Jesus was telling him, 'Buy
what we need for the feast,' or to give something to the poor. (30)
So once he had received the piece of bread, that man left at once.
And it was night.

This passage contains the first use of the designation "the disciple whom Jesus loved."[11] This mysterious figure, not otherwise
named, appears several times from here on and is identified in
the Appendix as the author of the Gospel (21:24). His importance
in the Gospel lies not only in his being an occasional eyewitness
of Jesus' last days (there is no suggestion that he was present
earlier), but also in his privileged intimacy with Jesus. This is
deftly signaled by his location at supper. Ancient Mediterranean
people preferred to recline at banquets rather than sitting in
chairs. The usual couch was large enough for two persons, though
sometimes longer benches might accommodate more. Whichever
was the case at this dinner, the beloved disciple was lying immediately in front of Jesus, with his back to him, both of them
at an angle to the table. It was the ideal position for a private
conversation that would not be overheard.

The beloved disciple learns who the betrayer is—but also seems
to know a good deal more. When Jesus gives Judas the piece of
bread soaked in the juices of some platter, it is as if the psalm
verse cited before is fulfilled all at once. Judas chews Jesus' bread
and immediately becomes his irrevocable enemy. Satan had already prompted Judas to betray Jesus (13:2), but now he takes full
possession of the betrayer. One might almost say that Judas becomes transparent now to Satan in the way that Jesus' disciples
are transparent to Jesus and, through him, to the father. Thus,
once Judas has left, John tells us, "it was night." These last words
deftly characterize what Judas has done; he has abandoned the
light. Now he cannot but stumble.

The narrative aspect of the Last Supper is now largely told; but
there is still a great deal to be said. In the narration, we have
passed back through the stages of the Christian life: new life,
enlightenment, Eucharist, Baptism, conversion. What is gained
in them can also be lost. Judas's departure into the night undoes,
for him, everything that the son came to give. Yet, there are others

who are still struggling to believe; Jesus has more to tell them, for the new life within the cosmos is not the final stage of the believer's progress. Jesus' crossing over to the father will make possible a new reality in the life of the believing community, and Jesus now prepares the faithful for it.

8

UNION II

(John 13:31—14:31)

Jesus is now departing, but this does not bring his work to a close. He will continue to be active in and with his disciples through an all-encompassing love. Jesus' departure is necessary because of this love, the same love that he leaves with his disciples as a new commandment:

(13:31) So when he [Judas] had left, Jesus says, "Now the son of humanity has been glorified, and God has been glorified in him. (32) And God will glorify him in him; and he will glorify him at once. (33) Little children, I'm still with you a little while. You'll look for me; and just as I told the Jews, I now tell you: Where I'm going you cannot come. (34) I'm giving you a new commandment: to love one another—for you, too, to love each other just the way I've loved you. (35) This is how all people will know that you're my disciples, if you have love for one another."

"Glory" is metaphorically related to "light." (Note how they are interwoven above in 12:27–36.) Jesus' glory, the power and beauty of his connection with God, stands in sharp contrast now to that night into which Judas has just departed. He does not first receive his glory at this time; it was his from the beginning (1:14) and he revealed it in his signs (2:11). This glorification is rather a reemergence and a reaffirmation of his ultimate reality, now moving rapidly to completion. One aspect of it is love (to be taken up again later); another is that Jesus will now move beyond the confines of this cosmos—in the first instance, through death.

(13:36) Simon Peter says to him, "Sir, where are you going?" Jesus answered, "Where I'm going, you cannot follow me now; but you'll follow later." (37) Peter says to him, "Sir, why can't I follow you now? I'll lay down my life for you!" (38) Jesus replies, "You'll lay

down your life for me?! Amen, amen, I say to you, not a rooster will
crow till you deny me three times.

Peter correctly senses that Jesus is speaking of his death and
insists that his own loyalty would carry him even there with
Jesus. He is right, of course, in the long run, but not in the immediate context. What he is really expressing just here is not
loyalty to Jesus, but the disciples' disinclination to let Jesus go.
The necessity of his going must now be a theme:

> (14:1) "Don't let your hearts be disturbed. Believe in God; believe
> in me, too. (2) In my father's house, there are many places to stay.
> If there weren't, would I have told you that I'm going to prepare a
> place for you? (3) If I do go and get a place ready for you, I'm coming
> back and I will take you to myself so that where I am, you, too, may
> be. (4) And you know the road to where I'm going." (5) Thomas says
> to him, "Sir, we don't know where you're going. How can we know
> the road?" (6) Jesus says to him, "*I* am the road and the truth and
> the life. No one comes to the father except through me. (7) If you've
> known me, you'll know the father, too; and from now on you do
> know him and you've seen him."

Jesus' death is not an accident of history but a fundamental step
in the return of the creation toward the creator. The reasons for
this will be expressed in a great variety of ways; to begin with,
John has Jesus speak here in quite concrete terms about preparing
places in the father's house. The language seems vaguely apocalyptic: certain things must be done in heaven before events can
proceed on earth. Yet, for John, this is more metaphor than literal
reality. Jesus has already, as God's logos, created the places where
humanity lives on earth; now, through his human obedience and
glorification, he is creating a new kind of humanity in a new
relationship with God. He himself is the road to real life—a life
which brings one face to face with the father.

> (14:8) Philip says to him, "Sir, show us the father and we'll be sat-
> isfied." (9) Jesus says to him, "Have I been with you all this time,
> Philip, and you haven't known me? The person who has seen me
> has seen the father. How can you say, 'Show us the father'? (10) Don't
> you believe that I'm in the father and the father in me? The words
> I speak to you I don't speak on my own; but the father, staying in
> me, does his works. (11) Believe me, because I'm in the father and
> the father in me; otherwise, believe because of the works
> themselves.

Jesus is not only humanity's road to God, but God's road to
humanity. In him the two meet, so that to see him is to see the

father. Only through enlightenment can one grasp this, and even now the disciples find it difficult. The person of true insight believes this simply because it is true. Jesus would accept even a lesser form of belief, that based on "the works themselves"; but the enlightened person will not have to reason from the external evidence of signs. The enlightened look at Jesus and see the father.

In any case, the works are not primarily proofs; they are simply the expressions of God's power and goodness through those united with him. As such, they will not cease with Jesus' departure, but will be communicated to others by it and even enhanced:

> (14:12) "Amen, amen, I say to you, the one who believes in me—that one, too, will do the works that I do, and will do greater works than these because I'm going to the father. (13) And anything at all that you ask in my name, I'll do it, so that the father may be glorified in the son. (14) If you ask me anything in my name, I'll do it. (15) If you love me, you'll be keeping my commands. (16) And I'll ask the father, and he'll give you another sponsor to be with you for ever, (17) the spirit of truth. The cosmos can't receive it, because it doesn't see it or know it. *You* know it because it stays with you and will be in you.

Jesus' reunion with the father will grant a new access to God's power, so that Jesus' followers will be able to perform works even greater than his—but only insofar as they are really his followers. Jesus promises that he will do "anything at all" that they ask (it is the expression Mary used at Cana, 2:5)—but provided they ask in his name. This means that every request must proceed from love, for that is the commandment that he has given them at the beginning of the present discourse (13:34–35). As long as they are truly his, the father, at Jesus' request, will supply them with "another sponsor" *(paraklētos)*.[1] Jesus has been their sponsor before God up to now (and, in a sense, will continue to be); but his departure does not deprive them of sponsorship. It simply changes its form. Hitherto, it has been limited to a historical and geographical presence. (This is why the arrival of the Greeks in 12:20–23 was so important. Jesus' influence, during his ministry, could expand only by the normal social channels and only gradually reach the necessary groups.) Now, it takes the form of spirit, equally accessible in every time and place to those who believe.

The spirit, here, is not exactly another "person," except perhaps in the sense that Jesus is other than the father. As Jesus makes the father present, the spirit will make Jesus present:

(14:18) "I won't leave you bereft; I'm coming to you. (19) A little while now and the cosmos sees me no more; but you go on seeing me, because I am alive and you will be alive. (20) On that day you will know that I am in the father and you are in me and I in you. (21) The one who has my commands and keeps them—that's the one that loves me. And the one who loves me will be loved by my father; and I will love him and show myself to him." (22) Judas, not Iscariot, says to him, "Sir, what's happened that you're going to show yourself to us and not to the cosmos?" (23) Jesus answered and said to him, "If anyone loves me, he'll keep my word. And my father will love him, and we'll come to him and make a place to stay with him. (24) The one who doesn't love me doesn't keep my words. And the word [logos] that you're hearing isn't mine; it's the father's who sent me.

The cosmos seems now to be moving beyond the possibility of salvation, but that is perhaps not quite accurate. "Cosmos" has, all along, been John's word for the creation in its alienation from God. John never held out any hope that Jesus would effect a complete reversal of this condition, but only that he would give some people the right to become God's children. In one sense, Jesus has already shown himself to the cosmos. As he leaves the cosmos, however, through his death, resurrection, and ascension, that presence is no longer available in the same way. With the believers alone, he can now speak of a new kind of presence, consisting in the mutual indwelling of father, son, and believers.

One term for this is "life." Jesus is "the road and the truth and the life." Therefore, to be truly alive is to participate in what Jesus is. The believers will go on seeing him "because I am alive and you will be alive." Another word for this new way of being is "love." Love offered to one another (Jesus' commandment) is also love offered to Jesus and is met by an answering love from Jesus and the father, which is their true self-revelation. The disciples do not understand this, perhaps because they are not yet truly living in it. (Jesus does not actually give the spirit until later, 20:22.) They continue to think in terms of public, social, historical ministry; and this brings the "other" Judas to ask why Jesus has changed his plans and is now writing off the cosmos.

Jesus replies with an "inappropriate response," which seems at first to have nothing to do with Judas's question. Yet, it is the only possible answer to it. Jesus will show himself to the believers alone because they are the only ones who can see. And they can see only because they love and are loved. To love one another is

to love Jesus; to love Jesus is to love the father; to love them is
to see them and to live with them and to be loved by them. This
is the logos that was from the beginning—not simply Jesus' word
(logos, v. 24) but the father's.

The transition from the one mode of Jesus' presence to the other
is not easy. That is why Jesus is telling them about it beforehand.

(14:25) "I've spoken these things to you while I'm still with you;
(26) but the sponsor, the holy spirit that the father will send in my
name—that one will teach you all things and remind you of all that
I've said to you. (27) I leave you peace. My own peace I'm giving to
you. I'm not giving to you the way the cosmos gives. Don't let your
hearts be disturbed or fearful. (28) You've heard what I've said to
you: 'I'm going away and I'm coming to you.' If you loved me, you'd
be glad that I'm going to the father, because the father is greater than
I. (29) And now I've told you before it happens, so that whenever it
does happen, you may believe. (30) I'll not talk much with you again,
for the ruler of the cosmos is coming. And he has no share in me,
(31) but it's so that the cosmos may know that I love the father and
do just as the father has commanded me. Get up; let's leave here.

The disciples cannot understand their new life in love until
they receive the new sponsor, the spirit—until they are actually
living the new life. Jesus has told them before, to ensure their
sense of continuity, but the spirit will bring to them the understanding of what Jesus meant. Jesus' departure is actually a great
gift to the disciples—the gift of peace. This is not a gift of the
cosmic order, something created and perishable, but a gift of the
divine order, distinct from all their previous experience. Jesus
draws it from the father who is "greater than I" and it will be
communicated through the spirit "that the father will send in
my name." How, then, can Jesus' departure be a terror to them?

This is not to deny that there is a terrifying element in the
events to come. The ruler of the cosmos (Satan?) is coming. Jesus
will fall under his power to kill and destroy. But this happens not
because the cosmos has any real power or authority in relation
to Jesus; it is only to prove to the cosmos how meager its powers
are. This passion and death cannot break the bond of unity, the
love and obedience that hold father and son together. The fundamental presupposition of the prologue, that God and logos are
one, will be demonstrated gloriously on the cross. The first discourse at the supper thus ends by stressing the unity of father
and son.

The last words of the discourse, however, are puzzling. They seem to bring the supper to an end as Jesus and the disciples rise from table; yet, Jesus will go on speaking, without any major interruption, for three more chapters. It has been suggested that the first discourse might originally have stood alone. The second discourse covers much of the same ground and could be an expanded version which our author intended to substitute for the first one. For some reason, the two came to stand side by side instead; and whoever placed them thus failed to remove a few now-inappropriate words between them. Although this explanation seems plausible, it is still perplexing that the author or editor should have failed to make so simple a correction.[2]

I would suggest that it was not absent-mindedness that allowed the words to stand, but rather their structural usefulness and their susceptibility to a mystical reading. Structurally, they mark the division between the two discourses, which would otherwise be hard to catch. This division is important for the reader precisely because the second discourse will rework material from the first and the reader needs a sense of a new beginning in order not to become badly disoriented. Mystically, the words can be read as an announcement that Jesus is about to move to a new level of speech. They can be translated, in this secondary sense, "Wake up; let's go on from here." The second discourse will be more explicit about John's mystical doctrine and its consequences for life here and now. This does not mean it will be any clearer. Is mystical speech ever "clear" except to those who have experienced some little of the reality behind it? It means, however, that the reader must read alertly.

9
UNION III
(John 15:1—17:26)

The reality of all existence lies in its intimate relationship with the father through the son. This existence comprises everything that is, insofar as it is in love with its creator. Yet, the creation has another aspect in which it stands in opposition to its creator and its own true life; it is this that John calls "the cosmos." When Jesus restores the relationship of love between God and his disciples, he does not take them physically out of the cosmos. They live, now, in and from God's love, yet also in opposition to the predominant state of their world. Why does Jesus not simply take "his own" with him and leave the cosmos to its own devices? Because the cosmos is, in principle, salvageable. Cosmos is not a thing, but a disposition. The creation is good in being (which is a gift from God), and evil only in its stance of alienation from God. The disciples must now stay in the presence of the cosmos in order to testify to it about the truth.

This is the central thread of the second discourse. Jesus begins it with a strong reaffirmation of the disciples' utter dependence on him:

(15:1) "*I* am the real vine, and my father is the farmer. (2) Every branch of mine that doesn't bear fruit—he cuts it off; and every one that does bear fruit—he cleans it up so that it will bear more fruit. (3) You're already clean because of the word I've spoken to you. (4) Stay in me, and I in you. Just as the branch can't bear fruit on its own unless it stays in the vine, neither can you, unless you stay in me. (5) *I* am the vine, *you* are the branches. The one who stays in me and I in him—this one bears much fruit, because apart from me you can't do a thing. (6) Unless a person stays in me, he's been thrown out, like the branch, and withered. And they collect the branches and throw them into the fire, and they get burned. (7) If you stay in me and my words stay in you, ask whatever you want and it will happen for you. (8) This is how my father has been glorified, so that you bear much fruit and become my disciples: (9) just as the father has loved me, I, too, have loved you. Stay in my love. (10) If you keep my commands, you'll stay in my love, just as I've kept my father's commands and stay in his love.

(11) "I've told you these things so that my joy will be in you and your joy will be brought to the full. (12) This is my command: to love each other the way I've loved you. (13) No one has a greater love than this—to lay down one's life for one's friends. (14) *You* are my friends, if you do what I command you. (15) I'm no longer calling you 'slaves,' because the slave doesn't know what his lord is doing; but I've called you 'friends,' because I've let you know all the things that I've heard from the father. (16) You didn't choose me; but I chose you and set you to go out and bear fruit and your fruit to last, so that anything at all you ask the father in my name, he'll give you. (17) I'm giving you these commands: to love one another.

The image of the vine is a vivid illustration of the disciples' dependence on Jesus: apart from him they are dead; in him they live and produce fruit. There is a threatening note in Jesus' development of the image when he speaks of the possibility of being cut off and thrown into the fire. But this danger is not really new—only the obverse of his repeated insistence that the disciples must love him and keep his commands. Judas is the example of what happens to the one who fails. He was motivated not by love, but by greed (12:4–6), and ended in betrayal.

The point of the metaphor, in any case, is to produce not fear, but joy (v. 11). Jesus raises his disciples from the status of slave to that of friend. He does this by dying for them. Yet, this joy is not some private possession for the disciple. To join the company of friends means to love one another, and Jesus' sacrifice becomes the model for all behavior. Only the branch that bears fruit may remain on the vine.

The mere existence of such a community bound to one another and to the father through the love of the son is an affront to the cosmos, for the cosmos represents the opposite mode of life, that of hatred and alienation.

(15:18) "If the cosmos hates you, you know that it hated me before you. (19) If you belonged to the cosmos, the cosmos would love its own; but since you don't belong to the cosmos (but I have picked you out of the cosmos), this is why the cosmos hates you. (20) Remember the word that I spoke to you: 'A slave isn't greater than his lord.' If they've persecuted me, they'll persecute you, too. If they've kept my word, they'll keep yours, too. (21) But they'll do all these things to you because of my name, because they don't know the one that sent me. (22) If I hadn't come and spoken to them, they wouldn't have sin; but now they have no excuse for their sin. (23) The one who hates me hates my father, too. (24) If I hadn't done among them the works that no one else has done, they wouldn't have sin; but now they've both seen and hated both me and my father. (25) But it is to fulfill the word written in their law: 'They hated me for nothing.'

(26) "When the sponsor comes whom I'll send you from the father, the spirit of truth who issues from the father, that one will testify about me. (27) And *you* will testify, too, because you've been with me from the start.

(16:1) "I've told you these things so that you won't stumble. (2) They'll exclude you from the synagogue; but an hour will come when everybody who kills you will think he's doing God a service. (3) And they'll do these things because they haven't known the father or me. (4a) But I've told you these things so that when their hour comes you'll remember them—that *I* told you.

The Johannine community had apparently passed though some bitter times and probably expected still more to come. While one can only speculate about the nature of these events, the residue of bitterness suggests that they consisted of internal conflicts within the Jewish communities to which the Johannine Christians belonged. They resulted in the expulsion of the Christians from the official structure of the Jewish community and perhaps even in the deaths of some.[1] The Jewish nation, between the two great Jewish wars, was in a state of radical reconstruction, forced upon it by the loss of its old political and religious center and by an uncertain prospect of survival. In such circumstances, passions are easily aroused and differences of belief become the basis for mob actions and sometimes for quasi-legal violence as well.

In the present passage, it is clear that John thinks of the hostile "cosmos" as made up primarily of Jews, for he mentions expulsion from the synagogue as one form of its assault on the disciples and describes a psalm quotation as coming from "their law." Yet, he does not call the opposition here "the Jews," and that is highly important. For John, the ethnic or religious identity of the persecutors of his own day was theologically irrelevant. Under other circumstances, they might as easily have been Greeks, or Romans, or Scythians. What characterizes the persecutors theologically is that they are "the cosmos," the creation rejecting its creator. The effect of Jesus' work is to sharpen this opposition. The cosmos is no longer merely drifting along in its darkness. A flash of light has revealed where it is going. "The light has come into the cosmos and people have loved the dark more than the light, for their acts were evil" (3:19). Now, the alienation of the cosmos from God is more and more a matter of full choice, and the disciples must expect to be persecuted energetically and with purpose.

The cosmos is not one neatly defined group of people over against another. It was easy for John to look at his own community, tiny and oppressed as it was, and see in it little of the evil that characterizes the cosmos. But he never lets the reader forget who Judas Iscariot had been before his betrayal of Jesus. Any group that can persecute and kill people and think it is doing God a favor is a manifestation of the cosmos. The distinction is not between two human religious communities, but between two ways of being, one admitting the reality of God's primacy and living out of the father's love, the other arguing for its own primacy and living on hatred for any that deny it.

If the disciples are to be exposed to this hatred, they will also be supported by the assurance of God's reality and of Jesus' continuing gifts to the believers.

(16:4b) "Now, I didn't tell you these things from the start, because I was with you. (5) But now I'm going to the one that sent me. And none of you is asking me, 'Where are you going?' (6) But because I've told you these things, sorrow has filled your hearts. (7) But I'm telling you the truth: it's to your advantage that *I* go away. For if I don't go, the sponsor won't come to you; but if I do go, I'll send him to you. (8) And when that one has come, he'll convict the cosmos on the points of sin and justice and judgment: (9) sin, because they don't believe in me; (10) justice, because I'm going to the father and you no longer see me; (11) judgment, because the ruler of this cosmos has been judged.

(12) "I still have many things to tell you, but you can't bear them now. (13) But when that one, the spirit of truth, comes, he'll guide you in all the truth; for he won't speak on his own, but will tell all that he hears and will announce to you the things that are coming. (14) That one will glorify me, since he'll take from what is mine and announce it to you. (15) All the things that the father has are mine; this is why I've told you that he takes from what is mine and will announce it to you.

Jesus' departure, as already suggested, is more like a change in the mode of his presence. The spirit is in some sense "another," but brings nothing to the believers that has not already belonged to Jesus and to the father. Jesus' departure seems to be an occasion of sorrow, but only his sending of the spirit will really complete his work, confuting the claims of the cosmos once and for all. However much the cosmos denies it, its sin has become evident now in its rejection of Jesus, for God's work is to believe in the one God has sent (6:28–29). The cosmos also proclaims its own commitment to justice. But Jesus' departure to the father will be effected by this "justice," which thus proves to be mere legalized violence. This "justice" means, by an impossible twisting of the truth, the exclusion of love from the cosmos. Finally, the cosmos declares that it has the right to pass judgment; but in truth it has only the right to be judged. And that judgment has already been pronounced—on the one hand, in the cosmos's persistent love of darkness and fear of light (3:19); on the other, in Jesus' triumph of love and obedience leading to the cross. "The ruler of this cosmos has no share in me!" (14:30).

The cosmos has thus violated truth on all counts; but the spirit is the very essence of truth and leads the believers in it. In pointing them back toward Jesus, it also points them forward to the things to come:

(16:16) "A little while and you see me no more, and again a little while and you'll see me." (17) So some of his disciples said to each other, "What is this that he's telling us, 'A little while and you don't see me, and again a little while and you'll see me' and 'Because I'm going to the father'?" (18) So they said, "What is this 'little while'? We don't know what he's talking about." (19) Jesus knew that they wanted to ask him, and he said to them, "Are you debating with each other about this—because I said, 'A little while and you don't see me, and again a little while and you'll see me'? (20) Amen, amen, I say to you, you'll cry and mourn, and the cosmos will be glad. You'll grieve, but your grief will be turned into joy. (21) When the woman is giving birth, she's in pain because her hour has come; but when she gives birth to the child, she no longer remembers the suffering because of the joy that a human being has been born into the cosmos. (22) So you, too, have pain now. But I'll see you again, and your hearts will be glad, and no one takes your happiness away from you. (23) And on that day, you won't ask me for anything. Amen, amen, I say to you, if you ask the father anything in my name, he will give it to you. (24) Up to now, you've not asked anything in my name: ask and you'll receive, so that your happiness will come to the full.

The disciples will have to face the apparent collapse of their hopes when Jesus dies and is buried. The inner realities of the spirit are sometimes at variance with external appearances in the cosmos. Yet, his absence is not permanent. They will see him again, not only in the resurrection appearances, but with that special insight which comes from sharing in his life (14:19). Indeed, their closeness to him then will be such that it gives them direct access to the father in a way hitherto not possible. This means the completion of their happiness, the reaching of that goal, implicit in the creation itself, that everything should come from and return to the father in love.

It is only at this point of realization that it will be possible to speak directly about reality and to drop the figures of speech that characterize all this-worldly efforts to speak of it:

(16:25) "I've told you these things in figures of speech. An hour is coming when I'll no longer speak to you in figures, but I'll tell you openly about the father. (26) On that day, you'll ask in my name; and I don't say to you that I'll ask the father for you, (27) for the father himself loves you, because you've loved me and have believed that I came out from God. (28) I did come from God and I came into the cosmos; again, I'm leaving the cosmos and going to the father." (29) His disciples say to him, "See, now you're talking openly and not uttering any figure of speech. (30) Now we know that you know all things and don't need any one to ask you. This is why we believe that you've come from God." (31) Jesus answered them, "Do you believe now? (32) Look, an hour is coming and it's here already for you to be scattered, each of you to his own, and to leave me alone. And I'm not alone, because the father is with me.

(33) "I've told you these things so that you'll have peace in me. In the cosmos, you have suffering; but be brave—I've conquered the cosmos."

The disciples mistakenly think that they are already at the point of realization and they greet Jesus' words (in fact not much different from those he has used before) as the promised "plain speaking." They also optimistically proclaim their belief in Jesus. Jesus corrects them much as he corrected Peter earlier (13:37–38)—by mockingly repeating their assertion as a question. He made the same kind of deflating response to Nathanael, too, at the beginning of this Gospel (1:49–50). Believers readily develop too high an opinion of themselves; ultimately, they have nothing that has not come as a gift from God through the son.

Jesus has not, in fact, dropped the use of figurative language— nor will he do so anywhere within the confines of this book. John, as a mystic, knows that there is no nonfigurative language in this life for the realities of which he wishes to speak. His Gospel is still a this-worldly document and so condemned to the use of the figurative. Jesus says only that "an hour is coming" when one can dispense with such devices. The nature of that hour is adumbrated in the prayer that follows. This prayer affords the plainest language possible about union with God and John's understanding of it; even so, it cannot be said to escape the figurative.

Jesus has concluded the discourse with a short summing up: his words have interpreted the meaning of coming events, not only his own "crossing over," but also the tribulations the disciples will face. Suffering in the cosmos can coexist, for them, with their having peace in the son, since they know of his victory. With this, John turns to the great prayer which sums up the whole goal of Jesus' work:

> (17:1) Jesus said these things; and he raised his eyes to heaven and spoke: "Father, the hour has come. Glorify your son, so that the son may glorify you—(2) just as you gave him authority over all flesh, so that all that you've given him he might give to them—everlasting life. (3) And this is everlasting life—to know you, the only real God, and Jesus Christ whom you sent. (4) I've glorified you on earth by finishing the work you've given me to do; (5) and now glorify me yourself, father, alongside yourself with the glory I had by your side before the cosmos existed.

The exchange of glory between father and son reaches back to God's initial gift to the son before the creation of the world. The son's work on earth has been an act of returning that glory, so that the father can again give it to him and he to the father. Jesus has also given this glory to people on earth, where it takes the form of everlasting life, which is, in turn, the same thing as knowing father and son—knowing them, not merely knowing *about* them. This is the essence of the prayer—the perfection of glory (that is, of divine power and beauty) in the sharing of it.

Jesus goes on to speak of his work and his departure—and of the task left to his followers:

> (17:6) "I've revealed your name to the people you gave me out of the cosmos. They belonged to you and you gave them to me; and they've kept your word. (7) Now they know that all the things you've given me are from you, (8) because I've given them the words that you gave me and they themselves have accepted them and really know that they came from you. And they've believed that you sent me. (9) I myself am praying for them. I'm not praying for the cosmos, but for those you gave me, because they're yours. (10) And all things

that are mine are yours, and yours are mine; and I've been glorified in them. (11) And I'm no longer in the cosmos, and *they* are in the cosmos, and *I'm* coming to you. Holy Father, keep them in your name which you've given me, so that they may be one just as we are.

The prayer is focused on glory, but that does not mean it is concerned narrowly with Jesus or the father. The disciples are the principal subject of Jesus' prayer, and he prays for his own glorification because of what it means for them. They are God's own, given by God to Jesus; for just as no one can approach the father except through the son (14:6), so no one can come to the son except by gift of the father (6:65). And because they are the father's own, Jesus now entrusts them to him again; for as John said in the prologue, it is to those who are born of God that he gives the right to become God's children (1:12–13). The believers now recognize that they are from God, not from the cosmos. Yet, they are remaining in the cosmos while Jesus leaves it. All the more, then, is it important that the father keep them in his name, for this means that they will be like God—a likeness expressed here, rather delicately as yet, in the phrase "they may be one *thing* just as we are" (cf. 10:30). The oneness here is a oneness within the group of believers. No doubt it is the living expression of Jesus' command to love one another. Yet it is described as analogous to the unity of father and son. It is not, then, a creaturely quality, but a divine one.

The believers require this divine life because they must stay in the cosmos to continue Jesus' own mission:

(17:12) "While I was with them, *I* kept them in your name which you gave me, and I guarded them, and not one of them was destroyed except the son of destruction—so that the writing might be fulfilled. (13) But now I'm coming to you, and I'm saying these things in the cosmos so that they'll have my own happiness brought to the full in themselves. (14) *I've* given them your word, and the cosmos has hated them because they're not from the cosmos, just as *I'm* not from the cosmos. (15) I'm not praying for you to take them out of the cosmos, but to keep them out of the evil. (16) They aren't from the cosmos, just as *I'm* not from the cosmos. (17) Consecrate them in the truth: your word is truth. (18) Just as you sent me into the cosmos, I, too, have sent them into the cosmos. (19) And on their behalf *I* consecrate myself, so that they, too, may themselves be consecrated in truth.

The believers face a difficult existence, exposed to the hatred of the cosmos and deprived of Jesus' immediate protection. They will be safe, though, as long as the father keeps them and consecrates them in the truth. This truth is God's word, that is, the message of Jesus in this Gospel, which leads one along the mystical path. As Jesus was in the cosmos as the full reality of God's presence—now the believers must be, too.

To do this, they must participate in the very life of God. That is the climactic message of John's Gospel:

> (17:20) "Not for these only do I pray, but also for those that believe in me through their word, (21) that they may all be one, just as you, father, are in me and I in you, that they, too, may be in us, so that the cosmos may believe that you have sent me. (22) And as for me, the glory you gave me, I have given them, so that they may be one just as we are one, (23) I in them and you in me, so that they may be completed into one, so that the cosmos may recognize that you sent me and have loved them just as you loved me. (24) Father, I want what you have granted me, that where I am they, too, may be with me, so that they may see my glory, which you gave me because you loved me before the foundation of the cosmos. (25) Righteous father, even the cosmos did not know you; but I've known you and these people know that you have sent me. (26) And I have made your name known to them and I will make it known, so that the love with which you've loved me may be in them and I in them."

At this passage, the commentator might best remain silent. Certainly, one must not suggest that what John has expressed in just these words can be reproduced in any others, or that one might somehow capture the meaning better or set it out more clearly in some prosaic paraphrase. It may, however, be permissible to lift out a few important themes and examine them, so that the reader, upon returning to the text itself, will be more conscious of their ramifications.

The first such theme is the insistence that the unity of believers with one another is nothing less than the unity of father and son before the creation of the world. This is the unity alluded to at the very beginning of the prologue, when John said both that the logos was with God and that the logos was God. Such a unity does not submerge the separate reality of the beings which enter into it; one can still speak of the logos as being *with* God. Yet, this union overcomes all possibility of estrangement, so that, as our Gospel has repeatedly emphasized, Jesus and the father are really one. The unity to which the believers are now called is that of the primordial glory, the beauty and power of the godhead, before the foundation of the cosmos. Yet, it is not an unrelieved oneness, which excludes whatever is distinguishable from God, for even "at first, there was the logos" (1:1).[2]

A second theme, however, insists that, even if this unity is identical with the glory that Jesus had with the father before the foundation of the cosmos, it is also something to be brought about in a new way through Jesus' ministry—and equally through that of his followers. Since the father created the cosmos, surely the cosmos could be expected to know him; but it did not. Only the son knows him and makes him known. This is why Jesus speaks of the believers being "completed into one," for it is a unity that must develop over time through knowing Jesus as the one sent from God. Those who have known Jesus in this way, in turn, become vehicles for others who believe "through their word." Jesus' prayer for the believers here ("That they may be completed," *hina ōsin teteleiōmenoi*) will also prove to be true for himself in his crossing over to the father again: his dying word will be *tetelestai* ("It's completed").

A third matter to note is that the unity of which Jesus speaks here is not, as in some mystical writings, a union simply of the worshiper and God. It is first of all the worshipers' unity with one another. No doubt this means unity within the church community; but it can scarcely refer to a simple matter of organizational unity. It is not, then, a matter of "church unity" in the modern sense, nor may we read the passage as if it had some interest in "church growth" (another modern phase), as if a single, enormous, worldwide Christian institution would somehow necessarily be a better witness for the Gospel or as if the evangelist were arguing for unity on grounds of its potential missionary effectiveness. Neither an institutional nor a missionary reading of the passage is suitable, for both ignore the importance of the first theme we have noted: the unity for which Jesus prays is the divine unity, not any unity characteristic of human communities. Still there is a powerful issue of witness involved in this plea for unity: just as it is Jesus' own oneness with the father which makes of him the road by which others may come to God, so it is the believers' unity with one another in him that actually makes the journey back to our divine origin.

While these reflections in no way replace the text from which they arise, they may assist the reader in returning to it with a new awareness of some of its complexity. If one were to try to point at the same reality at which the text is pointing in words somewhat different, but still basically Johannine, one might do it thus: All things issue from the original glory of God, but the cosmos has not known and loved its creator; to make himself known that creator has sent the logos, who is with God and even *is* God, who participates in that original glory and communicates it to this creation. The creation, by rejecting its creator, had become the dark and sinful cosmos; the incarnate logos has entered it with love to recall it to its true light. The way to that light is love: God's love to us through Jesus; ours to God through Jesus; ours to one another through Jesus. This love is the divine unity, reaching out in power and in beauty to make all creation one with God.

<table>
<tr><td>The Crossing
Over of Jesus</td><td># 10
UNION IV
(John 18:1—20:29)</td></tr>
</table>

Union with God and with one another is the goal of the mystical road. The language which tries to speak of it in chapter 17, however, is cast in the form of prayer that it may be so; we are not, perhaps, to conceive of its having happened already in the story itself. While John may have fore shadowed it in the figure of the disciple whom Jesus loved,[1] he seems to feel that true mystical union with the son (and thus with the father) had to wait upon Jesus' own departure and the giving of the spirit. The final chapters of John's Gospel are thus essential to its plan and not merely an imitation of prior models, such as Mark and Matthew.

New life, the life signaled by the raising of Lazarus, means death to the cosmos. It was precisely the raising of Lazarus, in John's Gospel, that sealed Jesus' fate (11:45–53). Both Jesus and the disciples knew that it was a time of danger, and it was just at this time that Jesus began to speak, however vaguely, of the imminent departure of the light (11:9–10). John may describe Jesus' departure variously as a "crossing over" from the cosmos to the father (13:1), as a "lifting up" on the cross (3:14; 8:28; 12:32–34), or, most frequently, as a glorification (7:39; 12:16, 23; 13:31–32; 17:1, 5). However it is described, it includes four main elements: death, resurrection, ascension (rather vaguely worked in), and the giving of the spirit. John does not seem to distinguish sharply among these in terms of their effects; all are aspects of one great movement, so that the lifting up is also an act of power and the glorification includes the death on the cross.

From the perspective of space and time, however, the events

109

are sequential and must be told one by one. In the telling, we shall see their conformity with all that has gone before. Sometimes John will remind us of earlier motifs; at other moments, the continuities are clear enough without his jogging our memory. The concluding narrative begins with Jesus' arrest:

(18:1) After saying these things, Jesus went out with his disciples across the Kedron wadi where there was a garden; he and his disciples went into it. (2) Now, Judas, who was betraying him, also knew the place, since Jesus had many times gathered with his disciples there. (3) So when Judas had gotten the cohort and some servants from the chief priest and the Pharisees, he comes there with lanterns and lamps and weapons. (4) So Jesus, knowing all that was coming upon him, went out and says to them, "Whom do you want?" (5) They answered him, "Jesus the Nazorean." He says, "I am he." (Now, Judas, too, who was betraying him, was standing with them.) (6) So when he told them, "I am he," they shifted backward and fell to the ground. (7) So he again questioned them, "Whom do you want?" And they said, "Jesus the Nazorean." (8) Jesus replied, "I told you that I'm he. So if you want me, let these people go." (9) It was to fulfill the words he had spoken: "I've not lost a one of the people you gave me." (10) So Simon Peter, since he had a sword, drew it and struck the high priest's slave and cut off his right ear. (Now, the slave's name was Malchus.) (11) So Jesus said to Peter, "Put your sword into its sheath. Shall I not drink the cup the father has given me?"

Jesus had said, in the shepherd discourse, that he would lay down his life for his sheep—not under compulsion, but voluntarily (10:18). This is a regal act, as is vividly apparent in this narrative of the arrest. The large group that has come out against him, including both the governor's soldiers (the cohort; six hundred men at full strength) and the Jewish police (who had failed to arrest Jesus previously, 7:45–46), is powerless against him. His mere admission of his identity overpowers them. Only his consent to be arrested allows them to proceed, and he still has power to save his followers—even the one who resorts to violence. This does not mean that Jesus is immune to suffering, only that the cosmos is powerless against him without his consent.

The detachment takes Jesus to the Jewish authorities:

(18:12) So then the cohort and the tribune and the servants of the Jews took him in charge and tied him up (13) and took him first to Annas, for he was father-in-law of Caiaphas, who was high priest that year. (14) (Now, Caiaphas was the one who had advised the Jews that it would be good for one man to die for the people.) (15) And

Simon Peter was following Jesus, along with another disciple. Now, that disciple was an acquaintance of the chief priest and accompanied Jesus into the chief priest's court, (16) but Peter was standing outside, by the gate. So the other disciple, the chief priest's acquaintance, went out and spoke to the gatekeeper and brought Peter in. (17) So the maid who was in charge of the gate says to Peter, "Are you one of this man's disciples, too?" That one says, "No, I'm not." (18) And the slaves and servants were standing there at a fire they'd made, since it was cold, and they were getting warm; and Peter, too, was standing with them and getting warm.

The account of Jesus' hearing before the Jewish authorities is so sketchy as to make little historical sense. There is nothing approaching a proper inquest, even to the degree that the Synoptic Gospels represent. Indeed, most of the enquiry takes place before Annas (perhaps the "power behind the throne" at the time), not Caiaphas, the legal high priest. So clumsy is John's arrangement of the material that he will actually have Jesus moved to Caiaphas's house before completing the story of Peter's three denials at the house of Annas (18:24–27).[2] One notes, in general, that John has very little interest in the other characters of this drama, with the partial exception of Pilate. We hear nothing of the fate of Judas Iscariot—or about any bargain between him and the authorities. We hear nothing about Peter's repentance after his denials. The Jewish authorities remain mere shadows. All this may suggest that John was a relatively clumsy author, but more significantly it tells us that his interests lay elsewhere: not on the narration of events, but on their relation to his overarching theological concerns. The spotlight is on Jesus' final conflict with the cosmos: on his own obedient and paradoxical victory and the futile violence of those who hate him.

It is for this reason that John includes the figure of the disciple who was an acquaintance of the chief priest. Such a person would have to have been at home in the aristocratic circles of Jerusalem. Perhaps he was not known to be a disciple (though the maid appears to have assumed that he was); more likely, his social standing protected him from arrest, even though he was accompanying Jesus. Perhaps he is the same person as the beloved disciple, who, alone among Jesus' male followers, was free to stand at the foot of the cross; or perhaps he was Nicodemus, who was a member of the Council. Whoever he may have been, he is here in the story not as historical reminiscence, but as ironic proof that the proud edifice of the cosmos has already been undermined. Even within its inner circle, there are those who have turned back to the creator.

Now that the cosmos has at last, as it supposes, gained the power to pass judgment on Jesus, it seems that it does not quite know how to proceed:

(18:19) So the chief priest questioned Jesus about his disciples and about his teaching. (20) Jesus answered him, "I've spoken openly to the cosmos; I've always taught in synagogue and in the temple, where all the Jews gather, and I've said nothing in secret. (21) Why are you questioning me? Question those who heard what I told them: see, these people know what I said." (22) But when he said these things, one of the servants standing nearby gave Jesus a blow and said, "Is this how you answer the chief priest?" (23) Jesus answered him, "If I've said anything wrong, testify about the wrong; but if right, why are you hitting me?" (24) So Annas sent him, tied up, to Caiaphas the high priest.

The decision to destroy Jesus was a political one (11:45–53), not a juridical one. The inquest is only the cosmos's effort to throw a cloak of justice over its procedures (cf. 16:8–11). Annas does not attempt to adduce any evidence against Jesus, but only invites him to incriminate himself. For Jesus, however, direct debate with the opponents is over; the important thing is what effect he has had on those who have listened to him. The same thing is implied by his words to the disciples at the Last Supper: "when the sponsor comes . . . that one will testify about me. And *you* will testify, too, because you've been with me from the start" (15:26–27). Even the cosmos could testify, if it would, since it has heard what Jesus had to say; even the servant who strikes Jesus could function as a witness.

The cosmos, however, will not witness, for to witness would also mean to confess its own alienation from its God. Even Jesus' chosen do no better in this critical hour:

(18:25) Now, Simon Peter was standing and getting warm. So they said to him, "Are you one of his disciples, too?" He denied it and said, "No, I'm not." (26) One of the high priest's slaves, who was a relative of the man whose ear Peter had cut off, says, "Didn't I see you with him in the garden?" (27) So Peter denied again, and at once a rooster crowed.

John is relatively sympathetic to Peter, making it clear that he was in real danger. He had committed an act of violence and was confronted by an eyewitness and relative of the victim. Yet, his failure is a minor episode. John does not encourage the reader to focus on Peter by describing his remorse; rather the removal of Peter as a participant simply underlines the centrality and the isolation of Jesus. Peter's failure confirms Jesus' earlier prediction (13:38), showing that every claim one makes for oneself, based on one's own courage or wisdom or devotion, is worthless. There is only one figure "in" the Gospel of John who can testify to his own worth—the father, who is the ultimate source of everything. Since the father is made present in Jesus, Jesus, too, is a figure of power—though repeatedly acknowledging his debt to the father. In the passion narrative, which tells of one aspect of his crossing over to the father, he is the only character of any real interest exactly because he is the only one truly in touch with the reality of all things.

The trial scene now shifts to the court of the Roman governor, Pilate. John gives a long version of Pilate's involvement with Jesus—and one that is not totally unsympathetic. Pilate, to be sure, is "of the cosmos" and ultimately consents to injustice; but he is at least troubled by it. There are even moments when his conversation with Jesus reminds one of a conversion dialogue, such as the one between Jesus and Nicodemus in chapter 3. Perhaps John is using this device partly to score points against his own Jewish adversaries, suggesting that the Gentiles came closer to doing justice than the Israelites. Still, in the last analysis, Pilate and Jesus' other opponents are in league; they all belong to the cosmos:

(18:28) So they take Jesus from Caiaphas into the governor's head-quarters. And it was early. And they themselves did not go into the headquarters building, so that they would not be polluted but might eat the passover. (29) So Pilate went outside to them and said, "What charge do you bring against this man?" (30) They answered and said to him, "If this man weren't doing wrong, we wouldn't have handed him over to you." (31) So Pilate said to them, "Take him yourselves, and judge him by your law." The Jews said to him, "We aren't permitted to execute anyone." (32) (This was so that the saying Jesus spoke, indicating by what sort of death he would die, might be fulfilled.)

Pilate's first public interview with the opponents is inconclusive. They will bring no public charges against Jesus; yet they are clear in indicating that they want Jesus executed. This will mean that Jesus will die by crucifixion, not a normal Jewish mode of execution, but commonly used by the Romans. John's community saw a particular significance in this mode of execution, since it involved "lifting up" the victim, suspending him between heaven and earth. Thus, Jesus' death will exemplify the full truth about him.

If the historical Pilate was initially reluctant to execute Jesus this must have been due to his fear of provoking riots just when the city was overflowing with the festival crowds—and perhaps also to a general disinclination to do the Jewish authorities any favors. John's picture, however, shows a theologized Pilate, as is already suggested here by the note that "it was early." Jesus was betrayed at night, that is, in the complete alienation of the cosmos from God. He is brought to Pilate very early, presumably before sunrise. The Romans did like to conduct business at this hour; but since John need not have specified an hour at all, the reference here probably has a symbolic aspect to it, suggesting that Pilate is at least hovering at the edge of understanding.

The remainder of the encounter between Jesus and Pilate is more dialogue than trial. The first part of it takes place in private:

(18:33) So Pilate went back into headquarters and summoned Jesus and said to him, "You—are you the king of the Jews?" (34) Jesus answered, "Are you saying this on your own, or have others told you about me?" (35) Pilate answered, "Am *I* a Jew? Your nation and the chief priests have handed you over to me. What have you done?" (36) Jesus answered, "My realm doesn't belong to this cosmos. If my realm did belong to this cosmos, my servants would have struggled so that I wouldn't be handed over to the Jews. But as it is my reign does not belong here." (37) So Pilate said to him, "Then you *are* a king?" Jesus answered, "*You* say that I'm a king. This is why I was born and this is why I came into the cosmos—to testify to the truth. Everyone that belongs to the truth hears my voice." (38a) Pilate says to him, "What is truth?"

Pilate's opening question shows that the authorities have privately denounced Jesus to him as a royal pretender, even though they have refused to bring the charge publicly. Jesus replies in much the same way as he did to Annas—by asking whether this charge is based on evidence. Pilate tacitly admits that the chief priests and other authorities have told him and that he has no other familiarity with the matter. Jesus responds with an equivocal statement about "my realm" and "this cosmos." The expression "my realm" could mean "the realm of which I am king" or "the realm to which I am subject." Jesus never refers to himself in John as "king"; but others do.[3] Thus Pilate makes the easy jump to concluding that Jesus' words are an admission of guilt;

but Jesus replies, "You used the word 'king'; I didn't." When Jesus himself previously spoke about kingship (3:3, 5), he referred to "God's realm." The father is the only true king; and Jesus has not in fact designated himself as such. (This is not, of course, for John merely a clever evasion; since Jesus is son and the son is one with the father, Jesus both is and is not king.)

The second point of ambiguity lies in the use of "the cosmos." We have already seen the specialized use to which John's Jesus has put the phrase: it does mean this creation, but most often only in its alienation from the creator. It is in this sense that Jesus' realm "does not belong to this cosmos" (literally, "is not from this cosmos"). And this is why Jesus' "servants" (note the echo of the "servants" of the authorities, that is, the police) do not fight; their command is to love, not to hate. Yet, "cosmos" also means "world," and Pilate, in his ignorance, will have to hear it that way. It appears to him, then, that Jesus is saying, "Yes, I am a king, but I don't exercise my power in this world." He is thus hardly a threat.

In any case, Jesus refuses to accept the title "king" or use it of himself. He will only say that he has come to testify to the "truth." Again, the richness which John has attached to the term is hidden from Pilate, who perhaps concludes that this is some kind of philosophical dispute and dismisses it with the skepticism of the man of action.

Still, he has no case against Jesus, and hovering as he is between Jesus and cosmos, he is still unwilling to execute him for nothing. He returns to his public role:

(18:38b) And once he had said this, he went out to the Jews and says to them, "I find no case against him. (39) But it's your custom for me to release one person for you at passover. Do you want me, then, to release 'the king of the Jews' for you?" (40) So they shouted back saying, "Not this man! Barabbas!" (Now, Barabbas was a robber.) (19:1) So then Pilate took Jesus and had him whipped. (2) And the soldiers plaited a crown of thorns and put it on his head and threw a purple cloak around him. (3) And they would come up to him and say, "Hail, king of the Jews!" And they gave him a beating.

Jesus is in the awkward position of one who cannot be acquitted because he has never been formally charged. Pilate could simply release him; but, fearful of mob violence, he wants to test the waters first. If there was a custom of releasing a prisoner (to add an extra occasion of joy to the festival), the mob gathered outside his headquarters must be understood to have come precisely to shout for their man. (John does not suggest that the authorities somehow subverted the mob.) Pilate is stymied, but apparently decides that the mob might be content with a lesser punishment for Jesus and he orders him whipped. The soldiers, taking their cue from Pilate's sarcastic reference to Jesus as "king of the Jews," make a mock king of him. (Whether or not there is much literal history behind the account, it is socially and politically plausible in terms of the period.)

It is Jesus, the king-not-king, whom Pilate will present again to the public as, at most, a crazy figure—certainly no threat to public order:

(19:4) And Pilate went back outside and says to them, "Look, I'm bringing him out to you, so that you will know that I find no case against him." (5) So Jesus came outside, wearing the thorn crown and the purple cloak. And he says to them, "Look at the fellow!" (6) So when the chief priests and the servants saw him, they shouted, saying, "Crucify! Crucify!" Pilate says to them, "Take him yourselves and crucify him, for *I* don't find any case against him." (7) The Jews answered him, "*We* have a law, and according to the law he should die, because he made himself God's son."

Jesus' regalia are appropriate to his kingdom, whose commandment is love; but in the terms of the cosmos, they are only a mockery of real kingship, which has to do with power expressed in violence. Pilate mocks Jesus in this way to suggest his powerlessness: "Look at the fellow!" Yet, this same Greek phrase also means, "See the human being," perhaps in the sense of the one real human being. Pilate's course is to evade judgment, but the opponents prevent him by leading the mob in a cry for blood. In the process, the cosmos reveals its true nature: it is derived from God but seeks God's destruction; it receives its life through the son and wants to kill him; it has a law which is God's gift through Moses (1:17) and uses that law against the one God has sent. Everything that the cosmos is and has is from the creator through the logos; but it is cosmos exactly insofar as it has turned on its maker.

Pilate has scarcely appeared to be a religious man, but he is standing in at least the first glimmering of the day's light, suspecting that there is more to Jesus than first appears. Accordingly, he senses, in the intensity of the antagonism between the authorities and Jesus, something frightening:

(19:8) So when Pilate heard them say this, he was more afraid, (9) and he went back into headquarters and says to Jesus, "Where are you from?" But Jesus gave him no answer. (10) So Pilate says to him, "You won't talk to me?! Don't you know that I have authority to let you go and I have authority to crucify you?" (11) Jesus answered him, "You'd have no authority over me at all unless it were given you from above. This is why the one that's betrayed me to you has a bigger sin." (12) After this, Pilate kept trying to release him, but the Jews shouted, saying, "If you let this man go, you're no friend of the emperor. Everyone who makes himself a king is opposing the emperor!" (13) So Pilate, once he had heard these words, brought Jesus outside, and he took his seat on the bench at a place called Stonepavement (in Hebrew, Gabbatha). (14) (Now, it was preparation day for the passover, about noon.) And he says to the Jews, "Look, your king." (15) So those people shouted, "Take him away! Take him away! Crucify him!" Pilate says to them, "Shall I crucify your king?" The chief priests answered, "We don't have any king except the emperor." (16a) So then he handed him over to them to be crucified.

Pilate, as a Gentile, may be a little readier than the Jews to believe that a human being might be a god's child. Whatever the source of his anxiety, he questions Jesus again. His assumption, like that of the Jewish authorities earlier (10:24), is that the question is one of simple and objective fact: "Are you the Christ?" "Where are you from?" In reality, the question, when it is framed thus, has no real answer. The issue is not so much where Jesus is from as where Pilate is from. Pilate claims authority to save and to kill; Jesus replies that that authority is not Pilate's in any important sense—it is from above. Jesus is immediately proven right, for Pilate now tries to save him—and proves incapable of doing so. The political maneuvering that has brought things to this point is no longer subject to his control. The cup Jesus will drink is the one that his father, not Pilate, has given him (18:11).

Pilate is stymied, ultimately, by threats to accuse him of being disloyal to the emperor, of turning a blind eye to the threat of sedition. He shifts his place of judgment, perhaps hoping to encounter a more favorable crowd. It is now the full light of day; Pilate has seen a measure of truth and uttered it.[4] Nothing helps, however. Finally, in order to ensure Jesus' death, the chief priests play their last card, and in the process, cast aside all pretense to belong to God: "We don't have any king except the emperor." The king they are denying is not so much Jesus as it is the father (though, for John, of course, the two are inseparable): their identification with the cosmos has reached full and explicit expression.

The result now is Jesus' execution:

(19:16b) So they took charge of Jesus; (17) and he went out, carrying his own cross, to what was called Skull Place (in Hebrew it is called Golgotha), (18) where they crucified him and two others with him, one on each side and Jesus in the middle. (19) But Pilate also wrote a placard and put it over the cross, and what was written on it was "Jesus the Nazorean, King of the Jews." (20) So many of the Jews read the placard, since the place where Jesus was crucified was close to the city and it was written in Hebrew, Latin, and Greek. (21) So the chief priests of the Jews said to Pilate, "Don't write 'King of the Jews,' but that that man said, 'I am King of the Jews.'" (22) Pilate answered, "What I have written, I have written."

Pilate has lost the power struggle, despite his extravagant claim to authority (19:10). He still gets a blow in at his political rivals by means of a placard he has put up—quite defensible in its wording, if their claims about Jesus' royal pretensions had been true, but acutely embarrassing to the sensibilities of a conquered people. It carries with it, too, at least the hint that the authorities have betrayed the one to whom they owed allegiance. When challenged by the priests, Pilate replies in oracular style, "What I have written, I have written." Like Caiaphas earlier on (11:51), he has become a kind of prophet—even a written, a scriptural one, for Greek makes no distinction of vocabulary between "writings" and "scriptures." Thus, the title that Jesus never claimed for himself becomes his on the cross—the right place and time for it, since it is one aspect of his leaving the cosmos and rejoining the true king, the father.

As in the Last Supper discourses, however, Jesus' departure does not signal any indifference on his part to the followers he leaves behind:

(19:23) So the soldiers, when they had crucified Jesus, took his clothes and made four portions, a portion for each soldier, plus the tunic. (Now, the tunic was seamless, woven in one piece from the top down.) (24) So they said to one another, "Let's not tear it, but let's draw lots for whose it'll be." (It was to fulfill the writing that says, "They have apportioned my clothes among them, and they have cast a lot for my clothing.") So, then, the soldiers did these things; (25) but standing beside Jesus' cross were his mother and his mother's sister, Mary of Clopas, and Mary the Magdalene. (26) So Jesus, when he saw the mother and the disciple whom he loved standing by, says to the mother, "Lady, see your son!" (27) Then he says to the disciple, "See, your mother!" And from that hour the disciple took her to his own place.

The early Christians were espousing an astonishing doctrine in claiming that a person who had suffered a shameful execution was God's anointed. Not surprisingly, they went to the sacred texts in an effort to prove that this was really what the faith of Israel had always proclaimed, even if interpreters had overlooked it. John has relatively few such scriptural citations. Perhaps he draws them from the tradition of his community. Perhaps he uses them to counterbalance the impression he sometimes gives that the writings belong only to "the Jews" and not, any longer, to the church (cf., for example, "your law," 8:17). We should expect, however, that when John does introduce a quotation, it will be adapted to his own primary interests. In this case, there is probably a reference to the baptismal mystery, as suggested by two points: first, the principal earlier reference to clothes comes in the footwashing episode, where Jesus took his clothes off to perform this service for the disciples (13:4); second, Jesus' tunic is described here as woven "from the top down," using the same Greek word (anōthen) used by Jesus in speaking to Nicodemus about baptism (3:3, where it was translated "again" or "from above"). This term is rare enough in the Gospel to catch the attentive reader's eye; and the connection with baptism would seem natural enough if the Johannine community, like other early Christians, baptized the converts naked.[5]

Jesus' death, as an act of love, is not an isolated incident affecting only himself. The baptismal allusion already suggests this, and the interchange with Mary and the beloved disciple confirms it. As Peter found, any reliance on the self excludes one from participation in Jesus' suffering and death; but those who know their dependence on the father through the son—such believers as Mary and the disciple Jesus loved—these may stand by the cross and receive Jesus' gift of love, which replicates itself in them. Mary has moved from being "his mother" to being "the mother," parallel to "the disciple," because the new familial relationship between the two establishes a pattern for the whole church.

Baptismal imagery now yields to that of the Eucharist as Jesus meets death:

(19:28) After this, Jesus, knowing that all things were now completed

for the writing to be fulfilled, says, "I'm thirsty." (29) A jug stood
there, full of sour wine; so they put a sponge full of the sour wine
on a hyssop twig and held it up to his mouth. (30) So when he had
accepted the wine, Jesus said, "It's completed." And he bowed his
head and handed over the spirit.

The earlier discussion of the Eucharist, in chapter 6, was focused primarily on the image of bread/flesh; this was dictated by
John's use of the feeding of the multitude as his point of departure.
The Johannine church's Eucharist, however, also included wine,
as the language about drinking Jesus' blood, later in chapter 6,
indicates. In the present passage, the wine is the ordinary rotgut
brought along for the executioners, and the scene (if one assumes
that even executioners have their moments of generosity) is plausible enough. Yet, it is no simple historical reminiscence, as the
reference to hyssop suggests. Since hyssop is a small, shrubby
plant (marjoram), it would hardly be useful in the way suggested
here (this, in fact, led some of the ancient copyists to revise the
passage so that it spoke of "wine with hyssop and gall," both
unpleasant flavorings). The reference to hyssop can only be a metaphorical one, perhaps alluding to its use as a purgative in preparation for the worshiper's approach to God (cf. Ps. 51:7).[6]

Jesus' acknowledgment of thirst is a highly charged matter, for
he earlier proclaimed to the Samaritan woman that "whoever
drinks from the water that I'll give him will never get thirsty
again to all eternity" (4:14). He also declared at the feast of Tabernacles, "If anyone is thirsty, let him come to me and drink"
(7:37). Just as his death gives life and his departure leads to his
return, so his thirst corresponds to the satisfaction of the thirst
of others; and the one who satisfied the wedding guests at Cana
with the best of wine must himself be content with the worst.
His suffering thus becomes the source of grace and truth, which
"came to be through Jesus Christ" (1:17).

This is what has been completed (teleō)—or fulfilled or accomplished or perfected. Jesus had spoken before about "completing
(teleioō) the work" the father had given him (4:34; 5:36; 17:4).
He has also spoken of the believers being "completed into one"
(17:23). His death attests to both kinds of completion: he is leaving his message behind him, both in words and in signs; he is
also inaugurating the possibility of the ultimate union by handing
over his spirit. He must go to the father before the spirit can come
to the believers.

The evangelist now recognizes in him the source of all grace:

(19:31) So since it was Friday, so that the bodies would not stay on the crosses on the Sabbath (for it was a high feast day on that Sabbath), the Jews asked Pilate to have their legs broken and the bodies removed. (32) So the soldiers came and broke the legs of the first who had been crucified with him and of the second. (33) But when they came to Jesus, since they saw that he was already dead, they did not break his legs, (34) but one of the soldiers stuck his side with a lance. And at once blood and water came out. (35) And the one who saw it has testified, and his testimony is true. And that one knows that he is telling the truth so that you, too, may believe. (36) For these things happened to fulfill the writing: "Not a bone of him shall be broken." (37) And, again, another writing says: "They will look at the one they pierced."

The beloved disciple (or so it seems) is claimed as witness of two final particularities of Jesus' death: that his legs were not broken (although those of the men crucified with him were); and that when he was stuck with a lance (to make sure he was dead), blood and water flowed out of the wound. Scriptural warrants are found for both of these details. Why were they important? The matter of the legs apparently served to connect Jesus with the passover sacrifices (cf. Exod. 12:46), which were presumably going on at the very time he was on the cross, although John never mentions them. This confirms that Jesus' departure is under divine protection, like that of the Israelites from Egypt, and that his death affords protection to those who are his own.

The blood and water might easily be a reference to the rites of Baptism and Eucharist.[7] (The order of the words is not necessarily against this; blood is mentioned first as the expected item, water second as the unexpected.) At this point, we can see that Jesus' crossing over is being paired in the passion narrative with the believer's earlier stages of progress along the mystical road. The trial before Pilate was a kind of conversion dialogue; the crucifixion and death are linked with the rites of Baptism and Eucharist. We may expect, then, that the stages of enlightenment and new life will correspond to further aspects of Jesus' return to the father.

First, however, the scene must be set; light, after all, becomes visible only in contrast to the preceding dark:

(19:38) Now, afterward, Joseph from Arimathea, who was a disciple of Jesus, but in concealment for fear of the Jews, asked Pilate to let him take Jesus' body; and Pilate gave permission. So he came and

took his body. (39) And Nicodemus came, too—the one who originally came to him at night—bringing a mixture of myrrh and aloe,
about a hundred pounds. (40) So they took Jesus' body and wrapped
it tightly with strips of cloth, with the aromatics, just the way the
Jews usually bury. (41) Now, there was a garden in the place where
he was crucified, and in the garden a new tomb, in which no one
had ever yet been put. (42) So because of the Jews' Friday, they put
Jesus there because the tomb was close by.

In a sense, these are the wrong people at work. Mary of Bethany
had already been appointed to supply the aromatics for Jesus' burial—and it needed less than a pound (though, admittedly, of very
expensive perfume) (12:7). What is more, there is something
wrong about both men: Joseph is only a secret disciple; Nicodemus originally came to Jesus at night—a sign of his lack of
enlightenment. They belong to that group of powerful people who
believed in Jesus but would not admit it because they loved
human glory more than the glory that God gives (12:42f). Their
belief is defective; and they wrap Jesus' body up tightly in the
cloth bands, much as Lazarus was wrapped (11:44), for they certainly expect no sudden reversal of his present state. They are
disciples—and also reminders of how inadequate disciples can be.

Yet, they have at least set the stage; and another will come,
also in the dark, to encounter illumination:

(20:1) Now, on the first day after Sabbath, Mary the Magdalene
comes to the tomb early, while it was still dark; and she sees the
stone moved back from the tomb. (2) So she runs and comes to Simon
Peter and to the other disciple, the one Jesus loved, and tells them,
"They've taken the lord out of the tomb, and we don't know where
they've put him." (3) So Peter went out—and the other disciple—
and they came to the tomb. (4) And they both ran together; and the
other disciple ran on faster than Peter and came to the tomb first.
(5) And he bends down and looks at the cloths lying there; yet, he
did not go in. (6) So Simon Peter arrives, too, following him, and he
went into the tomb. And he sees the cloths lying there (7) and the
handkerchief that had been on his head, not lying with the cloths
but rolled up into one spot apart. (8) So then the other disciple, who
had gotten there first, also went into the tomb and saw and believed.
(9) For they did not yet know the writing that he had to rise from
the dead. (10) So the disciples went back to their companions.

The Magdalene goes to the tomb in the dark and remains in
the dark through most of what turns out to be a long and, at first,
painful experience. The disciples are expecting nothing more of
the future than that it will confirm the past: that Jesus will remain

dead. This is how they show their lack of enlightenment. Jesus has been sufficiently explicit with them that he will return to them (14:3). If they do not expect his resurrection, that is because they do not really believe in the primacy of God nor in the centrality of Jesus in God's work. Without quite knowing it, they believe that the cosmos is more powerful than its creator. Therefore, Mary assumes only that the body has been stolen. The beloved disciple fears that graverobbers have ransacked the tomb and that there is still a corpse inside that might pollute him if he should touch it. Peter barges in, expecting to find something—anything—relevant to knowing what has happened. But they find only an absence: in the open tomb are empty graveclothes, evidence of a face uncovered first and then a body freed of its wrappings. That is what the beloved disciple came to believe at this moment—a real absence of the polluting corpse, no more. It all means nothing to them because they "did not know" the writings that prophesied the resurrection. Peter and the beloved disciple are as much in the dark as the Magdalene.

The Magdalene, however, stays by the tomb as an act of love—to lament, perhaps, but more especially to recover the body and see that it is properly buried, which was a fundamental religious duty:[8]

(20:11) Now, Mary was standing outside at the tomb, crying. So as she was crying, she stooped down and looked into the tomb, (12) and she sees two angels in white sitting there, one at the head and one at the feet, where Jesus' body had lain. (13) And those persons say to her, "Lady, why are you crying?" She tells them, "They've taken my lord away, and I don't know where they've put him." (14) After saying these things, she turned around the other way, and she sees Jesus standing there and did not know that it was Jesus. (15) Jesus says to her, "Lady, why are you crying? Whom do you want?" That woman, supposing he was the gardener, says to him, "Sir, if you've moved him, tell me where you put him, and I'll take him away." (16) Jesus says to her, "Mary." She turns and says to him in Hebrew, "Rabboni," which means "Teacher." (17) Jesus says to her, "Don't hold onto me, for I've not yet gone up to the father. But go to my brothers and tell them, 'I'm going up to my father and your father and my God and your God.'" (18) Mary the Magdalene comes, reporting to the disciples, "I have seen the lord"—and that he had told her these things.

What the mind rejects as impossible the eye can scarcely see or comprehend. Mary virtually ignores the angels and cannot recognize Jesus. She is at the opposite pole now from the enlightenment of the man born blind. He was willing to believe whatever Jesus told him; she can no longer even recognize Jesus when he stands before her—until he calls his own sheep by name (as he did with Lazarus, too). This is enlightenment and new life rolled into one. Jesus' new life is manifest to her, and her new mission releases her from her ministry at the tomb. Jesus' new life, however, is not simply a return to things as they were before. Jesus' life with the disciples in the cosmos is now near its completion and a new kind of relationship with God through the spirit must, as he promised, take its place. He had said that he would go to the father and send the spirit back to his disciples. Now, meeting Mary in the early hours of his risen life, he says, "Don't hold onto me" (perhaps even "Don't touch me"), for the old relationship with him as a person in space and time will not again be possible.

The new order now replaces the realities of Jesus' life and ministry, but at his own choice and as his own gift:

> (20:19) So when it was late on that day, the first day after Sabbath, and the doors where the disciples were were barred for fear of the Jews, Jesus came and stood right among them, and he says to them, "Peace be yours." (20) And having said this, he showed them hands and side. So his disciples were glad to see the lord. (21) So he said to them again, "Peace be yours. Just as the father has sent me, I, too, am sending you." (22) And having said this, he blew on them and says to them, "Receive holy spirit. (23) If you release the sins of any, they have been released for them; if you hold them, they have been held."

Jesus' appearance to the disciples brings them peace and gladness out of his own experience. He can show that he really is the one who went through suffering and death. Yet, he is present in an entirely new and glorious way. Even the newly risen Jesus required the opening of the tomb and came out of the graveclothes piece by piece. This is now the ascended Jesus, whose presence is somehow visible and tangible, but no longer constrained by the fleshly, created order. Thus he completes his crossing over and brings peace and gladness. This is not only a gift to the disciples, however, but a new life laid upon them. Jesus now sends them out in a way analogous to his own mission from the father; he empowers them with the spirit that binds them into the divine unity. "If I don't go, the sponsor won't come to you; but if I do go, I'll send him to you" (16:7).

John does not speak here specifically of union, only of the giving of the spirit and the sharing of God's prerogative to forgive sins. Earlier, he could have Jesus speak in the language of mystical union (chap. 17), for he was praying for something yet to come; nowhere, however, does John's Jesus speak of it as accomplished fact. Perhaps John did not believe that perfect union would come to pass in this life; and yet, his words about witnessing to the cosmos (17:21) would then seem pointless. Perhaps, then, he simply shared in the humility appropriate to the mystic, who is not to say, "This is mine." Indeed, one cannot say it because it is not; it is always gift and never possession.

What comes to the disciples, then, is holy spirit. Yet, this involves the power to save and to damn, to forgive and to withhold forgiveness. "If you release the sins of any, they have been released for them; if you hold them, they have been held." The terminology is technical: "releasing" and "holding" indicate the granting or denying of forgiveness. Jesus authorizes his disciples to act in this regard and declares that what they will do has already been ratified in heaven. In the hands of the cosmos, such powers would be used for destruction. In the hands of those who are truly Jesus' disciples, they can be used only for love. Therefore, what they do God has done in them.

In no way does this imply that the road from here on is easy or the story closed:

> (20:24) Now, Thomas, one of the Twelve, who was called "the Twin," was not with them when Jesus came. (25) So the other disciples were telling him, "We've seen the lord." But he said to them, "Unless I see the nail marks in his hands and put my finger into the nail marks and put my hand into his side, I'll never believe." (26) And eight days later, the disciples were again indoors, and Thomas with them. Jesus comes, though the doors were barred; and he stood in the middle of them and said, "Peace be yours." (27) Then he says to Thomas, "Put your finger here and see my hands, and take your hand and put it into my side. And don't be unbelieving, but believing." (28) Thomas answered and said to him, "My lord and my God!" (29) Jesus says to him, "Have you believed because you saw me? Blessed are those who have not seen and have still believed."

Here we come to the final episode of John's Gospel (not counting the appendix in chapter 21, which does not form part of the basic structure we are investigating in this study). It is a strangely unsatisfying conclusion—not a triumphant reunion, but a flawed one. In one respect, to be sure, it is just right. Thomas confesses Jesus with divine titles ("My lord and my God"), such as John told us from the first were appropriate. And his acclamation attests that Jesus' prayer has been heard and the father has glorified him "with the glory I had by your side before the cosmos existed" (17:5). Yet, it is an acclamation wrung from Thomas only by visible and tangible proofs. Such proofs are inappropriate at this point; the risen and ascended Jesus is no longer a creature of time and space. What is more, people who rely on signs are never truly reliable believers (2:23–25).

Yet, Thomas's weakness is, in a way, a sign of hope. One does not have to be the perfect mystic to be accepted among the circle of disciples. Even Thomas can still qualify; indeed, Jesus will make special concessions to confirm his faltering belief.[9] Even more than reassurance, however, Thomas's experience affords a continuing call to move along the road. The truest belief is that which arises from inner experience of the reality of God-in-Jesus, which yields a certainty and a blessing far greater than the evidence of the senses.

Jesus has now crossed fully over to the father. With the believers he has left peace, spirit, and a mission to the cosmos. Jesus' path has brought him out from the father and into the cosmos—and now out of the cosmos and back to the father. The believer's path, in a sense, coincides, for the believer, too, is "of God." Still, the way back to the creator is difficult for the inhabitants of this cosmos—even impossible without the road which Jesus' return opens up. The believer sets foot on it by steps that may be trivial and foolish, as in conversion, or grossly material and external, as in Baptism and Eucharist. But these are part of the same road that leads on to enlightenment, to new life, and ultimately to union both with God and with other believers. John is hesitant about claiming this unity as a fact fully realized here and now. Yet, he has given the reader to understand that it is given with the spirit, that it goes by the name of love, and that it is the essence of the church's being. Beyond it, apart from it, without it, there is nothing at all—not even cosmos; and its embodiment, as it comes to us, is Jesus, who is logos, son, lord, God.

11
EPILOGUE
(John 20:30–31)

Our author concludes his work with a brief note about the scope and purpose of what he has written:

> (20:30) So, then, Jesus did many other signs, too, in the presence of his disciples which have not been written in this book; (31) but these have been written so that you may believe that Jesus is the anointed, the son of God, and so that, as you believe, you may have life in his name.

This epilogue is explicit on two points: first, the work is not to be construed as a complete life of Jesus; second, the selection of things narrated has a theological purpose—to enable a belief which, in turn, will make life possible. In other words, the author's eye, throughout the book, has been as much on the reader as on the protagonist of the narrative.

Other authors of Gospels in antiquity did not apologize for the incompleteness of their works. Perhaps they regarded that fact as self-evident, or perhaps they did not wish to encourage comparisons, either with other books or with the continuing oral tradition about Jesus.[1] John, on the other hand, occasionally indicates that he expects his audience to know at least a little about the story from sources outside his own work.[2] Apparently, he felt no difficulty in acknowledging the existence of a larger tradition of which he was presenting only a selection.

Still, this does not explain why he should have felt the need to call attention to what must have seemed obvious to his intended audience. If there is a reason behind this confession (and one might expect an author's closing words to be products of conscious reflection), it is to claim that the *selection* of narratives is worth attending to, since it contains locked within itself the book's essential point. And if the selection is a kind of locked treasure, the words "believe" and "life" are the keys. The signs here narrated lead to the awakening or the strengthening of belief;[3] and believing leads to having life. The author aims to evoke one particular response in the reader, which he is confident will lead to a certain desirable result.

The vocabulary of this epilogue is highly characteristic of the Gospel as a whole, and a meticulous study of its use might well occupy as much space as the rest of this study put together. Without attempting so disproportionate an investigation, we shall at least need to look at the main outlines of the evidence, if we wish to grasp the sense of John's parting comments.

We can best begin with the verb "believe" (*pisteuō*; John does not use the related noun *pistis*, "belief," though I have occasionally employed it in my discussion): it occurs in all but two chapters of the book (15 and 18)[4] and is most often tied in some way to the person of Jesus. Sometimes it means trusting Jesus' reliability, as when he says to the woman at the well: "Believe me, lady, that an hour is coming . . ." Again, it may mean accepting what he says, as when Jesus asks, "Don't you believe that I am in the father . . . ?" Or, it may mean placing one's faith in Jesus, as in the oft-repeated expression, "the one who believes in me . . ." The last usage implies the other two and is a characteristic Johannine phrase, found more often in John and 1 John than anywhere else in the New Testament. But the phrase found in the epilogue ("to believe *that* Jesus is the anointed, the son of God") is not very different in meaning. To believe this statement, for John, is not to accept objectively the validity of a proposition, but to admit one's total dependence on the one who is incarnate in Jesus, the one who is the source and savior of all created existence. It implies a complete reassessment of one's relationship to reality, whether the subordinate reality of the cosmos or the ultimate reality of truth.

But what exactly does it mean, in human terms, to "believe"? I have traced, in John's Gospel, a portrayal of the believer's growth through a succession of stages: conversion, Baptism, Eucharist, enlightenment, new life, and union. What role does believing play in these? Is it the name of all stages or of one or a few only? If we look at the way John has used the verb earlier in the book, we shall see that, at the very least, "believing" covers more than one stage and that it is subject to refinement and growth.

When John deals with conversion, however, one can detect a certain wariness in his usage. After Nathanael has confessed Jesus as "son of God and king of Israel," Jesus asks ironically, "Because I told you that I had seen you under the fig tree, do you believe?!" (1:50). And Jesus himself does not "believe in" (or "trust"; the Greek is *pisteuō*) the people who believe in him, for they have not been transformed by their believing. Jesus' disciples, to be sure, "believed in him" after the miracle at Cana (2:11); but, later on, he will criticize belief that is dependent on signs (4:48) or external evidence (20:29). Conversion, then, may indeed be a kind of believing, but it is at most an early stage of it, dependent on external reinforcements, immature, and liable to reversal.

"Believing" can also have a baptismal reference, as in Jesus' conversation with Nicodemus. When Nicodemus misinterprets Jesus' words about birth *anōthen* ("anew" or "from above"), Jesus says to him, "If I've told you the earthly things and you don't believe, how will you believe if I tell you the heavenly things?" (3:12). "Earthly things" here seems to refer to Jesus' preceding proclamation about birth from water and wind or spirit. "Heavenly things" must look beyond baptism to the ultimate goal of Jesus' mission. Baptism, then, is an instance of "believing"; but, by itself, it is still only a preliminary.

Success at this early point in the believer's experience does not necessarily mean success later. Just as John casts doubt on the reliability of conversion (even when the convert, like Nathanael, agrees with John's own theology), so, too, in the story of the paralytic at the pool, he hints that the baptized may also turn back, even becoming traitors. Baptism, then, is an expression of believing, but it is not, in and of itself, the believing that gives life. We hear of such believing already in the section on baptism: "For God loved the cosmos so much, that he gave his only son, so that everybody who believes in him would not be destroyed but would have everlasting life" (3:16). Yet, Baptism is not of itself the believing that gives life.

Much the same can be said of the Eucharist, which John treats along parallel lines. Jesus emphasizes the importance of participating in this rite, as, for example, when he says: "*I* am the living bread that has come down from heaven; if anyone eats from this bread, he will live for ever. And the bread that I will give is my flesh—for the life of the cosmos" (6:51). An external rite, however, is not enough; to the same crowd, Jesus also says, "This is God's work—to believe in the person whom that one has sent" (6:29).

The rites are good and useful for what they convey, but they do not stand on their own. One of their functions is to screen out people who are incapable of proceeding further, that is, of acknowledging the real priority and centrality of Jesus. When Jesus uses the drastic language about chewing his flesh and drinking his blood, some find it a "hard saying." Jesus replies, "Does this make you stumble? What, then, if you should observe the son of humanity going back up where he was before. The spirit is what gives life; the flesh does no good at all. The words that I've spoken to you—they are spirit and they are life" (6:61–63). This is reminiscent of the earlier saying about "things earthly" and "things heavenly," which Jesus addressed to Nicodemus. The Eucharist has a positive role; but spirit and life are the real goals.

In the next section of the Gospel (enlightenment), the verb "to believe" is much less common, but it still plays a critical role. The blind man's spiritual awakening is captured in an interchange between him and Jesus about believing in the son of humanity. By letting Jesus become the arbiter of his faith, the man acknowledges his total authority. Those who do not believe can go no further: "if you don't believe that it is I, you'll die in your sins" (8:24). Yet, simply to believe (in the sense of conversion) is insufficient; and Jesus tells "the Jews that had believed in him, 'If you stay in my word, you're really my disciples, and you shall know the truth and the truth will set you free'" (8:31–32). Thus believing calls for a certain way of living, and that living produces the knowledge which, in turn, liberates. The same thought is put in a different way in the words: "The person who follows me will never walk in the dark, but will have the light of life" (8:12).

The gift of light, then, points on toward something more, whether it is described as "life" or as "liberation from sin." The gaining of this light may become manifest when one believes in a new way, as with the man born blind; but it is not to be identified with simple conversion or with the dependence on externals entailed in the receiving of sacraments. The believing that manifests enlightenment is rather the discovery and acknowledgment of our absolute dependence on Jesus, even though we know him imperfectly, for all comprehension of reality. Once one has grasped this, a real change of life must follow in that one is detached from the false claims and goals of the cosmos and attached to the true claims and goals of God.

This watershed between cosmos and God is the subject of John's section on new life, centered on the raising of Lazarus (and the prospect of Jesus' death). John treats this great miracle as an occasion for "believing," both for the disciples (11:15) and for the crowd (11:42); presumably, this use of the term covers all stages of the continuum, from conversion through enlightenment. Yet, John also applies the term specifically to the new life itself. In conversation with Martha, Jesus says, "*I* am the resurrection and the life. The one who believes in me, even if he dies, will live; and everyone who lives and believes in me will never die to all eternity" (11:25–26). Since Lazarus is already dead and since death in this world appears elsewhere in the Gospel as the norm for believers, it appears that believing is, in itself, the paradoxical entry into the new and indestructible life. There is no talk in John's Gospel of the human spirit living on after death, as if the flesh were only an appendix to our real humanity.[5] It is rather that the believer lives out of the truth, which is indestructible, and not out of the alienation of the cosmos. The one who believes (that is, embraces the truth) no longer fears death in this cosmos because of assurance arising out of God's absolute power and primacy.

Does one ever pass beyond believing? Is there anything beyond it that might be more certain or more secure? If even the new life that characterizes the believer in turning away from the cosmos is still a form of believing, must it not mean that all human experience of God still falls short of certainty? In a sense, yes. The fragility or inadequacy of belief is a topic that continues to exercise John right to the end of the Gospel. At the Last Supper, one of the disciples asks to see the father—evidence that he has still not fully believed that Jesus is in the father and the father in him (14:8–11). Later on, the disciples claim that they do believe, but Jesus replies that their own subsequent behavior will contradict them (16:29–32). Even after the resurrection, belief is difficult and incomplete and, for some, dependent on external demonstrations (20:29).

Yet, there are hints that one eventually passes beyond believing—by union with God in Jesus. This is perhaps only an occasional gift for the believer in this cosmos; but it is essential, from

John's point of view, since it is the verification of all else. One finds a new life in this cosmos as a result of enlightenment, but it is still a life of tribulation (16:33). At the beginning of his great prayer, Jesus declares that everlasting life consists in *knowing* the only true God and the one he has sent, Jesus himself (17:3). And the prayer goes on to ask, for the believers, not a strengthening of their belief but rather the experience of union with both father and son. Earlier in the Gospel, the terms "believing" and "knowing" seem roughly interchangeable as language about religious convictions. Now, belief drops into the background and knowledge comes to the fore—knowledge, moreover, as means to love, which is itself somehow equivalent to union: "I have made your name known to them and I will make it known, so that the love with which you've loved me may be in them and I in them" (17:26). Here is the conclusion of the prayer and also the goal of Jesus' whole mission.

In union, then, one passes beyond believing into knowing; and this knowing is everything Jesus had to give—that is, it is the same as everlasting life (17:2). One does not come, however, directly to this knowing or to this life. Believing is the path of approach, articulated by John into the steps of conversion, Baptism, Eucharist, enlightenment, and new life in the cosmos. The aim of John's writing, then, has been to encourage the reader along the path of believing in order to arrive finally at its end. Believe that Jesus is the anointed, the son of God—that is to say, recognize that all things, absolutely without exception, come from God through him and return to God through him. And thereby you will have life in his name, for returning to the father with him, you become one with him and with God and with all who have acknowledged that they belong to him.

APPENDIX
Secondary Passages

JOHN 7:53—8:11

(7:53) And every one went to his own home, (8:1) but Jesus went to the Mount of Olives. (2) Now, he arrived at the temple again early, and all the people were coming to him, and he took a seat and was teaching them. (3) But the scribes and Pharisees bring a woman arrested for adultery; and once they have stood her before everyone, (4) they say to him, "Teacher, this woman has been arrested in the very act of adultery. (5) Now, in the law, Moses ordered us to stone such women. So what do *you* say?" (6) (Now, they were testing him when they said this, so that they would have a charge to bring against him.) But Jesus bent down and wrote on the ground with his finger. (7) And when they went on pressing him, he straightened up and said to them, "The one among you who's never sinned is to be first to throw a rock at her." (8) And he bent down again and went on writing on the ground. (9) Now, the people who had heard started leaving, one by one, starting with the older ones; and he was left alone, with the woman before him. (10) So Jesus straightened up and said to her, "Lady, where are they? Has no one condemned you?" (11) She said, "No one, sir." And Jesus said, "I don't condemn you, either. Go; and from now on, don't sin any more."

JOHN 21

(21:1) After these events, Jesus revealed himself again to the disciples at the Sea of Tiberias; and this is how he did it. (2) Simon Peter and Thomas called "the Twin" and Nathanael from Cana of Galilee and the sons of Zebedee and two other disciples of his

133

were together. (3) Simon Peter says to them, "I'm going fishing."
They tell him, "We're all coming with you, too." They went out
and got on board the boat, and that night they caught nothing.
(4) Now, as it was just getting light, Jesus stood on the beach.
Yet, the disciples did not know that it was Jesus. (5) So Jesus says
to them, "Children, I don't suppose you have anything to eat?"
They replied, "No." (6) And he told them, "Cast the net to the
starboard, and you'll find something." So they did it—and did not
have the strength now to haul it in, it was so full of fish. (7) So
that disciple that Jesus loved says to Peter, "It's the Lord." So
Simon Peter, once he heard it was the Lord, tied his coat around
him (as he was naked) and threw himself into the sea.

(8) Now, the other disciples came in the boat, as they were not
far from land (only about a hundred yards), hauling the net full
of fish. (9) So when they got out onto land, they see a fire of coals
spread out and a fish and a loaf on it. (10) Jesus says to them,
"Bring some of the fish you've caught now." (11) So Simon Peter
went up and dragged the net onto the land, full of big fish, one
hundred fifty-three of them. And even though there were so many,
the net was not torn. (12) Jesus says to them, "Come have breakfast." And none of the disciples dared question him, "Who are
you?"—since they knew it was the Lord. (13) Jesus comes and
takes the bread and gives it to them—and the same with the fish.
(14) This was already the third time that Jesus revealed himself
to the disciples after being raised from the dead.

(15) So when they had had breakfast, Jesus says to Simon Peter,
"Simon son of John, do you love me more than these?" He says
to him, "Yes, sir, you know I have great affection for you." He
says to him, "Feed my lambs." (16) He says to him again, a second
time, "Simon son of John, do you love me?" He says to him, "Yes,
sir, you know I have great affection for you." He says to him,
"Take care of my sheep." (17) He says to him the third time,
"Simon son of John, do you have great affection for me?" And he
says to him, "Sir, you know all, you know that I do." Jesus says
to him, "Feed my sheep. (18) Amen, amen, I say to you, when
you were younger, you used to tie your own belt and walk where
you liked; but once you've gotten old, you'll stretch out your arms
and someone else will tie your belt and carry you where you don't
like." (19) (Now when he said this, he was indicating by what
kind of death he would glorify God.) And once he had said this,
he said, "Follow me."

(20) Peter turns around and sees the disciple Jesus loved following—the same one who reclined at his breast at dinner and said, "Sir, who is the one that's betraying you?" (21) So when Peter saw this man, he says to Jesus, "Sir, and what about this man?" (22) Jesus says to him "If I should want him to stay till I come, what business is it of yours? You follow me." (23) So this word got out among the brothers and sisters—that that disciple would not die. But Jesus did not tell him that he would not die, but "If I should want him to stay till I come . . ."

(24) This is the disciple who testifies about these things and has written these things, and we know that his testimony is true.

(25) There are many other things, too, that Jesus did—so many that if they were written up one by one, I don't suppose the cosmos itself would have room for the books being written.

NOTES

INTRODUCTION

1. Heracleon's commentary is preserved only in fragments cited in that of Origen. An English translation of the latter is found in Ante-Nicene Fathers; for Heracleon's fragments, see Robert M. Grant, ed., *Gnosticism: A Source Book of Heretical Writings from the Early Christian Period* (New York: Harper & Row, 1961), 195–208. The way Origen's own mysticism guided his reading of John is sensitively revealed by Patricia Cox, "'In My Father's House Are Many Dwelling Places': κτίσμα in Origen's *De principiis*," *Anglican Theological Review* 62 (1980): 322–37. For more extended modern discussions, see Maurice F. Wiles, *The Spiritual Gospel: The Interpretation of the Fourth Gospel in the Early Church* (Cambridge: Cambridge University Press, 1960), and Elaine H. Pagels, *The Johannine Gospel in Gnostic Exegesis: Heracleon's Commentary on John*, Society of Biblical Literature Monograph Series 17 (Nashville: Abingdon Press, 1973).

2. Even more catholic writers like William Temple were skeptical of mystical interpretations of John if they minimized the importance of Jesus. See Temple's *Readings in St. John's Gospel: First and Second Series* (London: Macmillan & Co., 1945), xx–xxi, 92–93.

3. C. H. Dodd, *The Interpretation of the Fourth Gospel* (Cambridge: Cambridge University Press, 1960), 10–53; David L. Mealand, "The Language of Mystical Union in the Johannine Writings," *The Downside Review* 95 (1977): 19–34; William J. Fulco, *Maranatha: Reflections on the Mystical Theology of John the Evangelist* (New York: Paulist Press, 1973).

4. Evelyn Underhill, *The Mystic Way: A Psychological Study in Christian Origins* (London: J. M. Dent, 1913); the quotation is from p. 241.

5. Rudolf Bultmann, in *The Gospel of John: A Commentary*, trans. G. R. Beasley-Murray et al. (Philadelphia: Westminster Press, 1971), treats about half of the instances of what I call the "inappropriate response" as evidence for literary dislocations or editorial seams.

6. E.g., when Tat, the initiand, asks, "Of what sort was the one born?"

Hermes answers in the future tense, "The one born will be distinct, God, child of God, the all in all . . ." (cap. 2). Since Tat thought he was asking about a past reality, he complains, "You are telling me a riddle, father, and not talking like a father with his son."

7. For surveys of recent discussion of sacraments in John, see Raymond E. Brown, *The Gospel According to John*, Anchor Bible, 2 vols. (Garden City, N.Y.: Doubleday & Co., 1966–70), 1: cxi–cxiv; Robert Kysar, *The Fourth Evangelist and His Gospel: An Examination of Contemporary Scholarship* (Minneapolis: Augsburg Pub. House, 1975), 249–59; C. K. Barrett, *The Gospel According to St. John: An Introduction with Commentary and Notes on the Greek Text*, 2d ed. (Philadelphia: Westminster Press, 1978), 82–85.

8. Of particular importance still in the discussion of sources is R. T. Fortna, *The Gospel of Signs: A Reconstruction of the Narrative Source Underlying the Fourth Gospel* (Cambridge: Cambridge University Press, 1970).

9. Kenneth Grayston, *The Johannine Epistles*, New Century Bible Commentary (Grand Rapids: Wm. B. Eerdmans, 1984).

10. Kurt Aland et al., eds., *Greek New Testament*, 3d ed. (New York: United Bible Societies, 1975).

11. John's language has been accurately characterized as an "antilanguage," which is likely to be falsified by being co-opted into a settled and dominant theological system. See Bruce Malina, "The Gospel of John in Sociolinguistic Perspective" (Center for Hermeneutical Studies in Hellenistic and Modern Culture, Protocol of the 48th Colloquy, 11 March 1984), 11–17.

1. PROLOGUE (JOHN 1:1–34)
THEOLOGICAL POSTULATES

1. Grayston, *Johannine Epistles*, 12–27.

2. See, e.g., the arguments of Brown, *Gospel According to John*, 1:18–23.

3. There was some uncertainty of interpretation even in antiquity, and Origen wisely insisted that this title of Jesus could not be made intelligible by itself. See Wiles, *Spiritual Gospel*, 65–66, 93–95.

4. See M. Jack Suggs, *Wisdom, Christology, and Law in Matthew's Gospel* (Cambridge: Harvard University Press, 1970).

5. Since the autograph of John's Gospel was probably unpunctuated, one could divide the sentences of vv. 3–4 differently: ". . . apart from him not one thing came to be. What came to be (4) in him (or, it) was life. . . ." There seems to be a modern preference for this alternative, but I think it is mistaken. The pleonasm of v. 3 serves to exclude all possibility of there being any creation at all apart from the logos; and "life" (v. 4) is not, from John's point of view, something created through the logos, but rather a property of the logos's own being (11:25; 14:6). Cf. the somewhat different argument for the same conclusion in Rudolf Schnackenburg, *The Gospel According to St. John*, 3 vols. (New York:

Crossroad, 1980–82), 1:239–40. For the ancient discussion, see Wiles, *Spiritual Gospel*, 71–76.

6. See the summary of the evidence in Raymond E. Brown, *The Community of the Beloved Disciple* (New York: Paulist Press, 1979), 69–71.

7. See C. K. Barrett, *The Gospel of John and Judaism* (Philadelphia: Fortress Press, 1975). Internal division of the Johannine community by "Judaizing" Christians may also have contributed to the usage; see Massey H. Shepherd, Jr., "The Jews in the Gospel of John: Another Level of Meaning," *Anglican Theological Review*, suppl. series no. 3 (1974): 95–112.

2. CONVERSION (JOHN 1:35—2:25)

1. For the problems in interpreting the phrase "lamb of God," see Barrett, *Gospel According to St. John*, 176–77.

2. The vast literature on the phrase "son of humanity" (or "son of man") appears to have reached an impasse. It is no longer possible to assume that the first-century Jewish or Christian audience would have recognized it as a familiar apocalyptic title. Here, in John 1, it may mean nothing more than "human being," the basic meaning of the Hebrew or Aramaic idiom being translated. In 9:36, John treats the phrase as if it were unfamiliar, at least as a technical usage, to the man born blind.

3. Reference to "the third day" in 2:1 serves to tie these two narratives to one another. Perhaps it also suggests that the second episode is to be evaluated positively in relation to the first, for the "third day," to a Christian ear, has the ring of resurrection about it.

4. Literally, "two or three measures" equals eighteen to twenty-seven gallons; but stylistic considerations demand round numbers here.

5. As Barrett notes (*Gospel According to St. John*, 191), the phrase "draws a sharp line" between Jesus and his mother; yet, its use does not automatically close a conversation.

6. Cf. 20:29: "Blessed are those who have not seen and have still believed."

7. I have preferred the singular *emeinen* ("he stayed") to the plural on literary grounds (because it is parallel with "he went down" and because it leaves open the issue of how long his family stayed) and out of the suspicion that it would have seemed untidy to scribes, who will then have "corrected" it. Use of a singular verb before a compound subject is easy enough, but not afterward.

8. Already in the third century, Origen argued that John had moved the narrative out of order so as to emphasize its inner meaning; cf. Robert M. Grant, *The Earliest Lives of Jesus* (New York: Harper & Row, 1961), 62–70. Most modern commentators agree, though William Temple showed that it is at least possible to argue in favor of the Johannine order; see *Readings*, 175–77.

9. Capernaum appears to be Jesus' Galilean headquarters in John's Gospel. He is "from Nazareth" (1:45), but does not visit there.

3. BAPTISM (JOHN 3:1—5:47)

1. Cf. 11:28, where Martha speaks thus of Jesus, and 20:16, where the Magdalene greets the risen Jesus as "Rabboni, Teacher." The title receives Jesus' approbation at 13:13.

2. One might compare the expectation, noted in Acts 8:14–19 and 19:1–7, that the Spirit would make its presence known at Baptism in observable ways.

3. In Greek, "everlasting" (aiōnios) has overtones of the "age" (aiōn) to come. It is John's equivalent for the more traditional Jewish and Christian phrase "reign of God," which he uses only in 3:3, 5.

4. The use of antlaō, "to draw," here and of a related word in v. 11 (antlēma, "bucket") carries the reader of the Greek back to the miracle at Cana. This may be a suggestion that the Samaritan woman is, like Mary, a true convert.

5. Note that John originally made the setting of this incident a "spring" (4:6), which itself suggests running water. Now, however, it has become a deep well (4:11) to contrast it to what Jesus can offer.

6. So Didache 7.2.

7. Hippolytus, Apostolic Tradition 23.

8. The Greek makes a play on words that is difficult to convey in English. The normal sense of the words would be to worship by spirit and truth, but the preposition used is the same as the one used above with "mountain" and "Jerusalem."

9. The words translated "labored," "worked hard," and "work" are all variants of the one translated "worn out" in 4:6, thus pointing to Jesus as the sower.

10. Any ritual immersion or solemn washing was a "baptism." Hebrews 6:2 suggests that early Christian catechesis included teaching to distinguish the central baptismal rite from other washings. Tertullian saw a baptismal reference here, according to Oscar Cullmann, Early Christian Worship (Philadelphia: Westminster Press, 1953), 84–85.

11. Some manuscripts have an additional verse (5:4), more or less as follows:

> For an angel of the Lord used to go down into the pool from time to time and stir up the water. So the first person to get in after the stirring up of the water would get healed of whatever sickness he had.

The addition may be traditional information, but was probably added to simplify the understanding of v. 7. It is unnecessary.

12. John's assessment of the sacraments is captured well by Ernst Käsemann: "John understands the sacraments as a possible encounter with the Logos and thus robs them of the kind of 'sacramental' quality usually associated with them." See The Testament of Jesus: A Study of the Gospel of John in the Light of Chapter 17 (Philadelphia: Fortress Press, 1968), 44–45.

4. EUCHARIST (JOHN 6:1—7:52)

1. Justin Martyr, First Apology 65; Hippolytus, Apostolic Tradition 21–23.

2. E.g., D. E. Nineham's discussion of Mark 6:30–44 in *Saint Mark* (Philadelphia: Westminster Press, 1977), 179.

3. The thought here is not far from Ignatius of Antioch's later description of the Eucharist as "medicine of immortality" (*Ephesians* 20.2).

4. The Twelve are seldom mentioned as such in John. There is no formal introduction of them; John assumes that the reader knows their significance as a group.

5. There is a reference to "disciples" in 9:2, but these could easily be Jerusalem converts. The next unquestionable mention of the Galilean disciples is the reference to Thomas in 11:16.

6. See, for example, *Aboth* 1. The "literature" in question (v. 15) would consist largely of what we now call "scripture." (There was no distinct word in ancient Greek for "scripture," and the boundaries of the canon were vague. Accordingly, I have used the vaguer English terms "writings" and "literature.") "Literature" will have been synonymous with learning; but the ancients seem never to have supposed that one could acquire an education from undirected reading. A teacher, who was also interpreter of the texts, was always necessary.

7. Note the present tense; though Greek can use present for future, the ambiguity here nicely expresses the mystery of Jesus' relationship with the father.

8. One might speculate whether there ever was, in fact, any such quotation. Jesus, after all, has his knowledge of "literature" directly from God (7:14–18), and his own authority is as great as that of the written word. The whole passage is difficult, in any case. The most lucid discussion of its problems I know is that of Barnabas Lindars, *The Gospel of John*, New Century Bible Commentary (Grand Rapids: Wm. B. Eerdmans, 1972), 298–302. It is odd, however, that previous commentators seem not to have observed that, as in the imagery of chap. 6 about eating human flesh and drinking blood, there is a strong element here of the reclaiming of what had been considered impure.

9. Note also Jesus' apparent reference to Judea as his "homeland" (*patris*), 4:44, and his ironic suggestion that the crowd does not know where he is from, 7:28.

5. ENLIGHTENMENT (JOHN 8:12—9:41)

1. The expression at the end of 8:25 is very difficult in Greek. In this context, it seems to mean something like "Just what I'm saying all along."

2. D. Moody Smith has also noticed elements of this relationship in *Johannine Christianity: Essays on Its Setting, Sources, and Theology* (Columbia: University of South Carolina Press, 1984), 202–3.

3. Since there is no clear trace of such excommunications of Christians before the First Jewish War (66–70 C.E.), this is usually taken to be an allusion to the situation of Christian Jews of John's own time. The anachronism, however, is not necessarily deliberate. Communities with few written records readily color their past with their recent experience.

4. Jesus identifies himself both here and to the Samaritan woman, 4:26, as "the one speaking with you." It is through what Jesus says more than

through miracles that one discerns the truth about him—and therefore about oneself and God.

6. NEW LIFE (JOHN 10:1—12:19)

1. The traditional English translations (e.g., "have it abundantly") seem to me to miss the note of excess in *perisson*.

2. Jesus' description of the verse as coming from "your law" is odd, since the Psalms belonged to the Writings, the least settled part of the Jewish canon, not to the Torah or Law. Either "law" had become a term for "canonical scripture" in the Johannine community or the group was beginning to lump all Jewish writings together in a somewhat hostile way.

3. Cf. chap. 5, n. 4, above; see also Käsemann, *Testament of Jesus*, 69.

4. Whether or not the Johannine tradition knew such miracle stories as the raising of Jairus's daughter or of the widow's son at Nain, John does not recount anything that would have prepared the disciples.

5. Caiaphas was high priest from about 18 to 36 c.e.—much more than just "that year." I suspect that John's language is a derogatory reference to the fact that he served at the pleasure of the Roman government, which might remove him at any moment.

6. Matt. 26:6–13; Mark 14:3–9; Luke 7:36–50.

7. UNION I (JOHN 12:20—13:30)
LOOKING BACK OVER THE
WAY WE HAVE COME

1. For the opposite possibility, that John means Greek-speaking Gentiles, see Brown, *Gospel According to John*, 1:314, 466. Yet, there is little other evidence that the Gospel is interested in Gentiles at all.

2. The Greek language may have assumed a particular importance to the Johannine community as it was being pushed out of the larger Jewish community. At some point after the First Jewish War (66–70 c.e.), Greek-speaking Jews were probably pressed to read scripture in Hebrew in their synagogues. The evidence for this is the existence of Hebrew texts written out in Greek letters to help with pronunciation. Origen made use of these in his *Hexapla*, but they were scarcely created for Christian use—and certainly not for people whose native tongue was Semitic. See Paul E. Kahle, *The Cairo Geniza*, Schweich Lectures 1941 (London: Oxford University Press, 1947), 86–87.

3. This seems to be the first time the author has introduced his own voice as a major interpretive device since 3:31–36.

4. 1 Cor. 11:23–26; Matt. 26:17–30; Mark 14:12–26; Luke 22:7–38.

5. For a survey of the issue of dating, see Schnackenburg, *Gospel According to St. John*, 3:33–37.

6. Cf. Heb. 10:22: "Let us come forward with a true heart in fullness of faith, as people who have been sprinkled in our hearts to deliver us from consciousness of guilt and washed in the body with clean water." There was a widespread tendency for early Christian exegetes to understand the person "who has bathed" here as the baptized; Georg Richter,

Die Fusswaschung im Johannesevangeliums (Regensburg: Pustet, 1967), 3–38.

7. George Nicol is surely correct in seeing the footwashing as a paradigm of John's descent-ascent Christology. See his "Jesus' Washing the Feet of the Disciples: A Model for Johannine Christology," *Expository Times* 91 (1979): 20–21.

8. Cf. 1 John 2:19: "They went out from among us, but they didn't belong to us. For if they had belonged to us, they would have stayed with us—but it was to make it obvious that not all belong to us."

9. Only here and in chap. 6 does John use the unusual verb "to chew" (*trōgō*). Enough of a point was made of it in the earlier chapter to make it stand out plainly here and resonate with the same themes.

10. Grayston, *Johannine Epistles*, 80–81, suggests that the Johannine community used the figure of Judas as a symbol of dissident groups. Origen made a similar connection; Wiles, *Spiritual Gospel*, 23.

11. Lazarus is described in 11:3 as beloved by Jesus, but he is not said specifically to be a disciple.

8. UNION II (JOHN 13:31—14:31)
FIRST DISCOURSE

1. Cf. 1 John 2:1: ". . . we have a sponsor with the father, Jesus Christ the righteous. . . ."

2. For ancient spiritual interpretation of the verse, see Wiles, *Spiritual Gospel*, 36–37.

9. UNION III (JOHN 15:1—17:26)
SECOND DISCOURSE AND PRAYER

1. For two influential efforts to reconstruct this history, see Brown, *Community of the Beloved Disciple*, and J. Louis Martyn, *The Gospel of John in Christian History: Essays for Interpreters* (New York: Paulist Press, 1978). While both these interpreters rightly emphasize the traumatic character of the Johannine community's expulsion from the synagogue (cf. also John 9:22), I am dubious of their detailed reconstructions. The Gospel appears to me to have been shaped by an overarching mystical conception which has left verbal traces of the community's history but hardly detailed historical documentation.

2. Käsemann, *Testament of Jesus*, 67–70, gives clear expression to the divine character of unity according to John's Gospel and sees it as constitutive of the Johannine church. At the same time, he remarks (p. 27) on the absence of an "explicit ecclesiology" from the Gospel. He is right in both cases. Mystical union is the life of the community, but permeates the visible church only imperfectly and does not allow for the construction of a detailed ecclesiology. Any ecclesiology of a genuinely Johannine character would have to rely heavily on modes of symbolizing, as distinct from fully incarnating, such unity in social institutions.

10. UNION IV (JOHN 18:1—20:29)
THE CROSSING OVER OF JESUS

1. The beloved disciple has often been understood as representing the true believer.

2. This seems to me the most natural reading of the passage, as it does to Schnackenburg, *Gospel According to St. John*, 3:239–40. It is possible, however, to understand the whole story as occurring at the palace of Caiaphas (the word I have translated "chief priest" more usually means "high priest"); see Barrett, *Gospel According to St. John*, 523–39.

3. Nathanael calls Jesus king in 1:49, and crowds see Jesus in that light in 6:15 and 12:13.

4. The emphasis on day and time in 19:14 may have signaled some ancient readers that the "trial" came to an end and Jesus was crucified at the time when the passover lambs were being killed. John, however, makes no reference to that event. At most, the phrase "lamb of God," used by John the Baptist (1:29, 36), might allude to it. The emphasis on passover is more likely to be linking Jesus' crossing over to God with the exodus from Egypt, while the hour (noon), being the time of brightest light, marks this as a transition into complete glory.

5. On baptismal nakedness, see Wayne A. Meeks, "The Image of the Androgyne: Some Uses of a Symbol in Earliest Christianity," *History of Religions* 13 (1973): 183–84.

6. See *Interpreter's Dictionary of the Bible*, s.v. "Hyssop," by J. C. Trever.

7. The associated quotation is from Zech. 12:10 and suggests that the violence of the cosmos will also be the beginning, by God's grace, of its repentance—something closely associated with Baptism.

8. Cf. the risks which Tobit took in burying the victims of political violence, Tobit 1:16—2:11.

9. Note v. 27: literally, "Don't become unbelieving . . . ," not "Don't be unbelieving. . . ."

11. EPILOGUE (JOHN 20:30–31)
JOHN'S PURPOSE IN WRITING

1. Werner Kelber, for example, has suggested that Mark wanted his written Gospel to take priority over oral tradition; *The Oral and the Written Gospel* (Philadelphia: Fortress Press, 1983), 90–131.

2. He assumes that they know who the Twelve and Mary of Bethany are, and he expects them to recognize allusions to the narrative of the institution of the Lord's Supper and perhaps to Bethlehem as Jesus' birthplace.

3. It is uncertain whether John used a present-tense verb in v. 31 ("that you may continue to believe") or an aorist ("that you may come to believe").

4. The verb *pisteuō* also does not appear in chap. 21. Early commen-

tators already recognized that the term has more than one meaning in John; see Wiles, *Spiritual Gospel,* 87–91.

5. Where John contrasts flesh and spirit sharply with one another (e.g., 3:6–8; 6:63), it appears to me that they are metaphorical for a merely external participation in rites as contrasted with an inner understanding and consent.

INDEXES

145

SUBJECTS

MODERN AUTHORS

ANCIENT BOOKS AND AUTHORS